"*The Epic of Gilgamesh* succeeds in revitalizing humanity's most ancient tale with a fresh take on the original text, enlightened by Kent H. Dixon's impeccable scholarship and brought to life by Kevin H. Dixon's skillful graphic storytelling techniques. Readers . . . will delight in discovering the creators' wry touches of humor and imagination as they reinterpret this classic saga in comics form."

—MATTHEW J. SMITH,
co-author of *The Power of Comics: History, Form, and Culture*

"This comic take on *Gilgamesh* offers readers a playful, action-packed, eminently readable new spin on this oldest of stories. Kent and Kevin Dixon imbue the ancient quest with a goofy, good-natured sense of fun, even as they evoke the subtleties of its timeless themes."

—ROLF POTTS,
essayist and author of *Vagabonding* and *Marco Polo Didn't Go There*

"An ancient tale refashioned in the style of underground comix from the 1970s, *The Epic of Gilgamesh* by the Dixons is the best kind of scholarly comic; one that is authentic, surprising, and accessible. Bringing contemporary readers to long forgotten lands and tales of adventure, *The Epic of Gilgamesh* is a welcome addition to the Graphic Canon."

—J.T. WALDMAN,
author and illustrator of *Megillat Esther*
and *Not the Israel My Parents Promised Me* (with Harvey Pekar)

"]A[monumental work, as well as a timely and therapeutic reminder that horrible flesh-eating monsters, great sex, and gargantuan egos have always been nestled comfortably within our collective DNA—and at 5,000 years old, the epic feels positively 21st century. I was blown away by what they have achieved."

—DAVID CATROW,
author and illustrator of the Max Spaniel series
and *When God Made You* (with Matthew Paul Turner)

The Epic of Gilgamesh

The Epic of Gilgamesh

TRANSLATED BY

KENT H. DIXON

ILLUSTRATED BY

KEVIN H. DIXON

SEVEN STORIES PRESS

New York • Oakland • London

A SEVEN STORIES PRESS FIRST EDITION

SEVEN STORIES PRESS
140 Watts Street
New York, NY 10013
www.sevenstories.com

Library of Congress Cataloging-in-Publication Data is on file

ISBN 978-1-60980-793-1 (pbk)
ISBN 978-1-60980-794-8 (ebook)

DESIGN
Stewart Cauley and Abigail Miller

Printed in the United States of America

1 3 5 7 9 8 6 4 2

CONTENTS

lovers and rejects her. Seeking revenge, she borrows the Bull of Heaven from her father Anu. It causes great devastation, but the heroes eventually slay it. Ishtar fumes; Enkidu throws the Bull's thigh in her face. The heroes are celebrated into the dawn, when Enkidu has an ominous dream of the gods.

TABLET VII

68

FOR THEIR ARROGANCE, "ONE OF THE HEROES MUST DIE." ENKIDU FALLS SICK, CURSES EVERYONE, IS REPRIMANDED BY SHAMASH, AND, AFTER 12 DAYS, HE DIES.

"One of the heroes must die," the gods decide. Humbaba, the Bull of Heaven, Ishtar . . . they have overstepped. Enkidu falls sick and curses everyone and everything that brought him to Gilgamesh. Shamash reprimands him for his ingratitude and he relents somewhat, but terrifying visions continue, of Anzu and the Netherworld. After 12 days, lamenting he is being denied a heroic death, he dies.

TABLET VIII

86

IN WHICH GILGAMESH LAMENTS, AT GREAT LENGTH, THE LOSS OF ENKIDU.

Gilgamesh is inconsolable. He calls on all the people, and all of nature, to mourn his friend. He recites their adventures; he blames himself. He tears his hair and rends his clothes; he commissions a great statue and concocts a funerary banquet for the gods.

TABLET IX

92

"IF ENKIDU CAN DIE, SO CAN I," REASONS GILGAMESH AND SETS OUT ACROSS THE DESERT TO SEEK REMEDY OF THE ONLY MORTAL TO HAVE BEATEN DEATH, ENCOUNTERING LIONS AND SCORPION MEN EN ROUTE. HE EVEN TRAVERSES SHAMASH'S TUNNEL.

While mourning his friend, it occurs to Gilgamesh that he, too, will die, so he decides to seek remedy from the "Faraway," Utnapishtim, the only mortal ever to have been granted immortality—the Babylonian "Noah," in fact. There are obstacles: a pair of lions attack—Gilgamesh now wears their skins. He comes to the sun god's tunnel, and must face down its guardians, the terrifying scorpion men. He traverses the tunnel and at the "12th double hour" he stumbles into Shamash's garden, all of jewels: "an entirely gemnified garden."

TABLET X

118

GILGAMESH COMES UPON SIDURI, WHO TRIES TO CONVINCE HIM THE SECRET OF LIFE IS NOT IMMORTALITY. BUT GILGAMESH FORGES ON AND WITH SIDURI'S DIRECTIONS, AND SOME WRONG MOVES, HE FINALLY FINDS UTNAPISHTIM, THE BABYLONIAN NOAH.
He comes upon Siduri, the solitary ale-wife at the edge of the sea. She fears him at first, but he tells her of Enkidu, and his own quest for immortality. She tries to dissuade him, but he is adamant, so she directs him to Urshanabi, the boatman who will ferry him to Utnapishtim. Muscling his way through, Gilgamesh destroys the "magic stones," the only means of crossing the Waters of Death. But with Urshanabi's guidance, he poles across to reach the Faraway, who advises him on death at some length before Gilgamesh recognizes who he is: "And I, Utnapishtim, am not dead." How so, asks Gilgamesh.

TABLET XI

138

UTNAPISHTIM RELAYS THE STORY OF THE FLOOD AND HIS UNIQUE SURVIVAL. BUT THIS IS NOT FOR GILGAMESH, WHO CAN'T STAY AWAKE FOR EVEN A WEEK. UTNAPISHTIM DOES DIRECT HIM TO A PLANT OF ENDURING YOUTH, BUT A SNAKE STEALS IT. GILGAMESH IS LEFT BOASTING OF HIS GREAT DEEDS AND THE WALL HE BUILT AROUND URUK.
Utnapishtim relays the story of the Flood (the same as in Genesis, but predating it by a millennium): the ark, the animals, the raven and dove, etc. The storm rages a week and wipes out the rest. The god who sent the flood is annoyed that one has escaped, but he's outnumbered, and Utnapishtim and his wife are rewarded with eternal life. But this can't be for Gilgamesh. As proof, Utnapishtim challenges him to stay awake for a week. He fails, but accepts their gift, a plant at the bottom of the sea that will make him young again, lifelong. Gilgamesh retrieves it (rocks tied to his feet), and sets out for home. But while he is bathing, a serpent steals away with the plant. For immortality, Gilgamesh can only boast of his great deeds, as he and Urshanabi approach the massive walls of Uruk.

Hisss

DEDICATED TO
RENÉE BARAT FANNON
OUR MOM & GRAND MOM

Reverse side of the newly discovered Tablet V of the *Epic of Gilgamesh*. Babylonian period, 2003–1595 BCE. It is currently housed in the Sulaymaniyah Museum, Iraq. It narrates how Gilgamesh and Enkidu entered into the Cedar Forest and how they dealt with Humbaba. (Photo by Osama Shukir Muhammed Amin. CC BY-SA 4.0.)

INTRODUCTION

WHAT WE HAVE here is the world's oldest story retold through one of the world's newest art forms. It's a meeting of the minds across the millennia. "From cuneiform to comix," as artist Kevin Dixon puts it.

Early versions of *The Epic of Gilgamesh*—an action-filled adventure that wrestles with life's big questions—were inscribed on clay tablets in Sumer as early as 2700 BCE. The fuller version that we're more familiar with was set down circa 1300–1000 BCE by a priest/scribe named Sîn-lēqi-unninni in Mesopotamia.

Some short works of literature were around earlier (such as maxims, spells, and brief poems from Egypt and Mesopotamia), but this is the first long work, and the first sustained written narrative, produced by the human race.

Meanwhile, comics are a relative newcomer to the world. Though there are some intriguing precursors, what we think of as comics sprang on the world in the early 1800s and didn't become widespread until late that century. In the history of art, this makes comics a toddler.

Gilgamesh follows the adventures, travails, and transformation of arrogant, insatiable god-king Gilgamesh of Uruk (modern-day Warka, in Iraq) and the wildman Enkidu. It's so visual—so brimming with monsters and gods and goddesses and bizarre landscapes and fight scenes and passion and emotion—it's a wonder that it hasn't been made into dozens of comics and movies. Into this gap steps the father-and-son team of the Dixons.

Until his recent retirement, Kent Dixon was a professor of literature and creative writing at a private liberal arts college, Wittenberg University, in Springfield, Ohio. His fiction and essays have been published in *TriQuarterly*, *Georgia Review*, *Antioch Review*, *Iowa Review*, and *The American Prospect*, among many other prestigious outlets, and have been nominated for the Pushcart Prize four times. Kent is also a literary translator, having brought Sappho, Baudelaire, Rilke, and other poets into English. When he decided to have a go at *Gilgamesh*, he went all in. By taking a distance-learning course from the Oriental Institute at the University of Chicago—with the oxymoronic course title "Cuneiform by Mail"—he learned about one third of the Akkadian syllabary in cuneiform symbols, the "alphabet" that Sîn-lēqi-unninni used to inscribe his *Gilgamesh* onto clay tablets.

Kent also worked with 30 previous English and French translations, creating a rendition in which he selected and modified from the best of the previous English editions, putting his emphasis on the humor and physicality of *Gilgamesh*. These aspects are plain in the original version, but scholarly types tend to sterilize ancient literature by putting it on a pedestal and cluttering it up with elaborate scholarship. Kent has given us a smooth and vibrant new translation/rendition with all the jokes, irony, raunch, action, and fun intact.

But instead of releasing this new, authentic version in the usual fashion, Kent asked his son Kevin to adapt it into comics form. With Kevin's specialty being vibrant, earthy, humorous comics, it was an obvious fit. Kevin Dixon is a 30-year fixture of the DIY underground comix scene, publishing much of his work, penning long-running strips in alt-weeklies, and scoring a Xeric grant in the process. He's risked the Man's wrath many times, from his early days printing his comics on the sly while working at Kinko's to taunting a certain corporation with *Mickey Death in the Winds of Impotence*. His well-known penchant for elaborate, perfectly rendered sound effects and homages to comics history serve the ancient epic well.

This ten-year *Gilgamesh* collaboration is a monumental project of comics adaptation, as well as a unifying experience for father and son. (I like that the original tale of male bonding has been turned into a comic by another male duo. But I won't try to figure out which Dixon is Gilgamesh and which is Enkidu.)

I found out about the existence of their ongoing *Gilgamesh* comic while assembling the original *Graphic Canon* trilogy. Part of my M.O. was to search online to see what was already out there. I would Google the name of a classic work of literature with the terms "comics" or "graphic novel" or "illustrated." When I did this with *Gilgamesh*, I was stunned to see that someone was already working on a faithful, unabridged adaptation.

Kevin was self-publishing *Gilgamesh* in installments. The available issues illustrated more

Tablet XI of the *Epic of Gilgamesh*.
(Photo by Osama Shukir Muhammed Amin. CC BY-SA 4.0.)

than half the tale, and he was getting close to drawing the entire thing. I nonchalantly bought two issues just to make sure it was as fantastic as it seemed. It was, and I immediately emailed Kevin. Deciding which portion of the epic to put in Volume 1 of *The Graphic Canon* was an agonizing decision (one of many for that project), but I finally went with the "Bull of Heaven" episode, and a cosmic panel from it became the book's cover. I knew this was a masterpiece in the making, and even then I was hoping that Seven Stories might publish the entire thing as a stand-alone work.

And here it is. Part *Odyssey*, part Hercules, part Ponce de León, part *Power Man and Iron Fist*, part *On the Road*, part bromance, part buddy movie . . . eons before any of those things existed.

RUSS KICK

TRANSLATOR'S NOTE

MY TRANSLATION OF the Gilgamesh epic is actually what is called a rendition, which is a translation made from other translations and not from the original. About half the "translations" out there of *Gilgamesh* (of the more than fifty in print, just in English) are renditions—including John Gardner's wild one, or the recently much-touted Stephen Mitchell's. That said, I did take a course in cuneiform taught by an Assyriologist at the University of Chicago's famous Oriental Institute, and I attempted to check my renditions against the original Akkadian (in cuneiform) wherever possible.

The institute's holdings are astonishing—actually awesome (some of the artifacts are 20 to 30 feet tall)—but the course itself transpired by email and snail mail, and in it I learned to read about a third of the 600 to 800 symbols that constitute the Assyrian syllabary, enough to allow me to hunt down individual words and even phrases in the 26-volume Chicago Assyrian Dictionary: does the wind "howl like an army passing over," or "scream like a woman in labor"? (Either is valid; I think I used both. The verb can also refer to trees rubbing each other, volcanoes rumbling, and Gargantuan fingernails grating across a blackboard (though that one's not in the CAD)). I also consulted more than two dozen translations in English, three in French, and one each in Italian and German.

I wanted a translation that would appeal to my college students and general readers, so my rendition tends to emphasize the story's sensory dimension. Hence, I call this "an enriched rendition," doing my best to dope it with a diction and vocabulary that evoke the most vivid sensory world. See Alexander Heidel's 1946 translation for something in English closest to the original Babylonian and Akkadian, and if you do that and compare it with other translations, you will see how much latitude scholars and poets take with this first piece of great world literature, both of necessity (the language is difficult, leaving much room for interpretation, and mistakes), and also oftentimes willfully: surprising how many hobby horses can dance on the edge of a tablet. My own effort, I maintain, while unabashedly biased toward the sensory world, is still one of the more accurate literally. Then, add the fun and insights of my son Kevin's drawings, and I propose we're giving a reader something like what the original audience experienced when it was read to them (and even possibly performed), capturing the range and sophistication of Sîn-lēqi-unninni's humor, pathos, horror, violence, and extraordinarily modern and candid "adult content."

We're thousands of years before Augustine's *Confessions* (and plenty of others, but he's the guy that screws us up the most about sex), and that time gap allows the overall tone of this work to be refreshingly natural, honest, and deeply, exquisitely human.

I would like to confess to one major fudge in my enriched rendition. In the original, Tablet XII begins with events that appear to be out of place after Tablet XI: Gilgamesh has returned home defeated but perhaps reconciled, while Enkidu is once again alive and seems more like a servant than any bosom-buddy. Scholars mostly agree that Tablet XII was a later addition to the epic, to give us a tour of the Netherworld, in which Gilgamesh eventually becomes a god. This twelfth tablet has been famously dubbed "the inorganic appendage," and the majority of translations simply leave it out!

But I had the great honor, when I was totally immersed in all things Gilgamesh, of meeting Sîn-lēqi-unninni himself (albeit in a dream), and he told me succinctly, and with great authority and patience, how to make the inorganic appendage organic. Quoth the ancient priest and scholar: "It's a dream, stupid."

Oh, and why not? The epic is rife with dreams. Tablet XII moves like a dream, plays with time like a dream, and, I'll tentatively propose here, it overlays and underpins—like Freud's concept of a dream's "latent imagery"—the epic tale that it concludes. I went to the actual tablet: the first nine or ten lines are either missing or are too damaged for even scholarly guesses. So, I supplied three of the missing lines from out of my own pocket. But who's to say they aren't so? Only Sîn-lēqi would know for sure.

KENT H. DIXON

ARTIST'S NOTE

I WAS MY FATHER'S second choice for this project. He originally wanted Julie Taymor to turn his rendition of *Gilgamesh* into a Broadway spectacle like *The Lion King*, with giant puppets and imaginative costumes and sets. After Taymor missed out on her big chance, making it into a comic book with me was the next best option. But maybe he should ask her again.

Back in 2000 CE, we began by sending copious notes, sketches, and rough page layouts back and forth through the mail. This took forever. Also, there were the agonizing decisions the artist has to make before embarking on a project of this scale. Once you commit to certain details, you can't change them one hundred pages in. Would I use Zip-A-Tone? I had only a limited stash, and it was becoming scarce and pricy on the black market. Now was not the time to graduate to the tools of the old masters, the brush and dip pen. I was too ham-fisted. A long way to go before developing something like a skill. Nor was it finally time to embrace the labor-saving technology we take for granted today. I didn't even have a computer! No, I would just carve this thing out on the cheapest Bristol board I could find, with my crappy unreliable Rapidographs and that maddeningly inconsistent nightmare in a bottle, Liquid Paper. Any shading in the art would be achieved by cross-hatching, a choice that just about cost me my eyesight.

I had grandiose plans to be historically accurate with the images, but was quickly disabused of that notion. You have to remember this story is told, re-told, revised, and enlarged across a couple of thousand years, by a procession of conquering civilizations. An Assyrian war helmet, which I like for its Smurf-like qualities, isn't necessarily going to look like the Sumerian-issue brain bucket from a millennium earlier. Oh, and here you've used a distinctively Akkadian hair style, yet the character is clearly riding an Old Babylonian chariot—which didn't even exist yet, so which is it?

The only contemporary visual references you get of the time are the monumental stone carvings and artifacts like those found in the tomb of Sargon II. Few are your glimpses of how the little people lived. Nobody commemorates what a toilet looks like on their Ziggurat of Triumph. I cribbed as many details as I could from art books and museums. I relied heavily on some pictures from things my dad sent, and especially on the images in a collection I found of old *National Geographic* articles from the 1940s and '50s, *Everyday Life in Ancient Times*, illustrated by H.M. Herget (who has to be doubly awesome for the hidden *Tintin* reference in his name). A trip to see the *Art of the First Cities* exhibit at the Metropolitan Museum of Art was an emotional experience for me. Not only was seeing the famous bull-headed lyre in person like meeting Pelé or Rod Stewart, but I felt deeply connected to the Ur-artists who had made this stuff. Hey man, I like your Gilgamesh. I'm working on a Gilgamesh, too! I wondered if these ancient colleagues of mine would enjoy working with Sculpey. I got a little choked up.

In order to get an exciting semi-self-contained episode to show around while I worked on the epic, I broke ground with the Bull of Heaven tablet. This would be fun to draw—it is one of the funniest tablets—and would let me hit the ground running for the long task ahead. I was most fortunate: the editor Russ Kick discovered it online, and included it in the first volume of his *Graphic Canon* series, leading to a long and fruitful relationship with Seven Stories Press.

There was, however, one drawback to starting in the middle of the story: wanting to change the middle once I finished drawing the beginning. The look of cartoon characters always evolves in the course of a long project. It used to drive me crazy, how weird Tintin and Astérix looked in their earliest appearances. Think of how different the Simpsons look in their first season, compared with the characters we know today. The Incredible Hulk, rivaled in his greenness by only Kermit the Frog and the Jolly Green Giant, was a sickly shade of gray when he made his debut.

You have to draw these characters hundreds of times before they achieve their classic streamlined look. I didn't do that. As a result, you get characters that look one way at the beginning, and fine for that, but then just as it appears the artist is finally working out the kinks in the design of his own cartoons they suddenly devolve into even rougher, more primitive proto-Gilgameshes and Enkidus than they were at the outset. Then, even more abruptly, while Enkidu is supposed to be sick and dying, the characters look healthier than ever. So the gradual morphing of refinement is out of order. It's like watching Mickey Mouse in *Fantasia* change into Steamboat Willie, and then instantly transform into today's fully-fledged corporate overlord rodent.

For a time, my dad and I considered the idea of a backstory, a sort of "Making of Gilgamesh" to weave into the epic. This would be an entertaining way to add footnotes, and some historical information, but would also parallel the story of Gilgamesh and Enkidu. My dad would be the cranky long-winded professor, Noah K. Samuelson, named in honor of the eminent Assyriologist Samuel Noah Kramer. I would be Lucky, the cranky degenerate cartoonist, named after Sîn-lēqi-unninni, the ancient scribe who gave us the most complete version of the epic. Hilarity ensues, but in the quest to achieve their great work, Enkidu's analog, Lucky—i.e., me—has to die. Eventually, in the surprise twist ending you never saw coming, we'd reveal that Noah K. Samuelson actually is Noah, as in Utnapishtim, the one man granted immortality by the gods. So my dad gets to be Gilgamesh AND Utnapishtim, while I get to be Enkidu, condemned to a dark and inky Netherworld? No fair! This "Making of" concept obviously needed some major revisions. But "Lucky" for me, the epic and all its characters ended up speaking for themselves. So my dad and I don't have to argue over which one of us is Enkidu and which one's Gilgamesh. (Trust me, nobody wants to be Enkidu.)

Besides, there are so many other characters we could identify with: Urshanabi the Boatman, who has the worst job in the whole epic, and gets yelled at and fired for doing it. Or Puzur-Amurri, the hardworking carpenter who helps build the ark, thinking he's hit the jackpot when he's given the "opulent palace and everything in it" for his labor by Utnapishtim, who in turn knows full well the whole thing will be twenty feet underwater before the weekend.

Or the one character who really seems to get it right: the tavern-keeper Siduri, who advises the Gilgamesh in all of us to slow down and enjoy the simple things in life, as they are meant to be enjoyed, and to not worry so much about stuff like immortality and whether or not your cartoon characters look too weird at the beginning. Hopefully this book straddles the line between Gilgamesh's ambition and Siduri's sensibility, by staying true to this oldest, greatest, and most human tale, and, more importantly, providing a simple pleasure in life—something you can enjoy.

KEVIN H. DIXON

The Epic of Gilgamesh

He who saw everything, did everything — you need his name?

The one who knew, and told us all these things, even of the days before the flood?

Whose journey was that but his — that wore him down to the marrow?

Whose story of that journey, carved in stone — and by whom?

Go on, touch it, climb upon it, inspect its ramparts. Its masons, you'd say, were the seven sages!
Here now, run your hand along this inner wall, grip the threshold here.
Go in: this temple called Eanna-Hush!— this holy place, more ancient than itself, yet fresh with divinity.

Look, you: this copper box. Pick its lock of bronze, lay agape its secrets...

...lift out the azure tablet of priceless lapis lazuli and read it yourself...
...of him who endured everything, him, whom they call Gilgamesh.

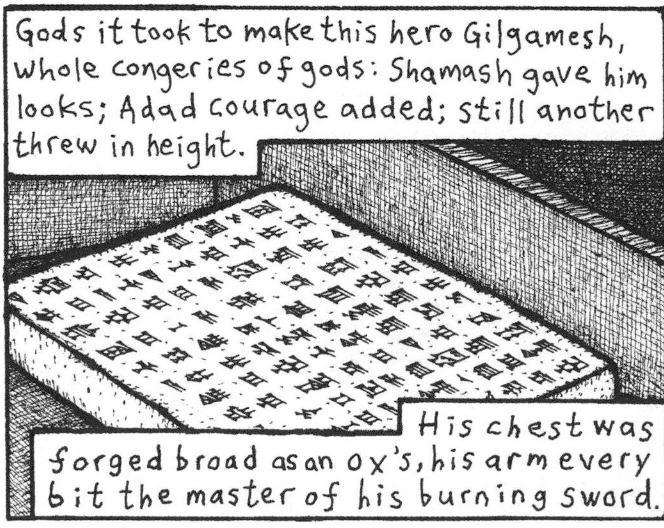
Gods it took to make this hero Gilgamesh, whole congeries of gods: Shamash gave him looks; Adad courage added; still another threw in height.
His chest was forged broad as an ox's, his arm every bit the master of his burning sword.

When they finished, he was only one third man,
two parts as heavenly as they.

Incomparable, matchless, and unsurpassed—and yet his people fret!

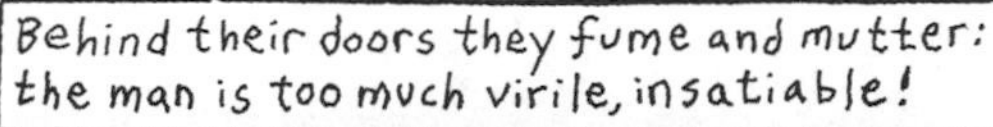
Behind their doors they fume and mutter: the man is too much virile, insatiable!

He claims "first night" with our virgin daughters—keeps them from their husbands, whether generals or wealthy noblemen!

Worse, for his work—and his play, too, no doubt!—he keeps sons from their fathers, even in the light of day.
KRAK

What's more, the temple drum—he pounds on it for sport!
BU-DOOM BOPBAP BOP BIPPETY BOOM DA BOP!

Such a one... our shepherd? Bold and wise, our handsome strong protector?
It's great to be me!

The gods, who frown on arrogance, heard these laments, and sent their own words stinging:
Anu!!
Anu, lord high, lover of Uruk City!
And thou Queen Aruru—Who created this beast?
Whose drum is he profaning? You like to skip to insolence?
Aruru made him. Now, let Aruru make his match.
Make one just like him, my dear, equal in appetite, even in strength. Let them fight, forever if need be—just so our Uruk gets a rest.

And Aruru, bowing her head indignant could think of only one – her husband – for a model. So in the likeness of the imperious Anu she began to mold her answer.

She spat on her hands, pinched off the clay, and cast it on the treeless plain, and then kneaded this lump into – it looked more like Ninurta, god of war!

The god of planting, too, primitive and shaggy, before men had ceased to eat the dirt. This man was hairy as an ape!

Hair ran down his back in waves, a woman's flowing tresses, or like a mane – so thick it swayed like fields of corn, and lay matted on his chest and arms. He looked like the god of yaks.

His dress was crude and coarse as shepherd's, though no shepherd he – ignorant of people and their feasts, no digger of rows, nor any need to herd a flock, nor idea how; instead, he ran with game...

UB GLUB GLUB BLUB!!

...ate grass with wild kine, drank water with just his lips; he needed hands but to clear space at river bank, slurping abreast his fellow beasts. What joy more, (he feels) to graze and drink beside gazelle?

A hunter saw him. Looked up one day across a stream and almost drew his bow: the barrow of fur stood up, man-tall, then gone! Young hunter was stunned.

He returned. A good day, his traps were full, but then again, not a leap away, this man of wooly curls – they stared. Young hunter was undone.

Third day, same thing, eyes that weren't quite human, yet weren't afraid. And now the animals were sprung, the hunter's line of traps were wrecked and strewn, hopelessly destroyed.

Which one the hunter here?

He went home speechless, looking broken, haggard, like *he'd* been living off the land and not this hairy other.

The hunter returned home with the paltry game he'd gathered...
Father! There's someone out there, some thing!

Maybe a god—he's as strong as one, but he eats with the animals, drinks at their water holes.
Go to Uruk, son.
You wouldn't go near him, but there he is in our woods!

He's torn up my traps! He's filled in the pits I dug.

You understand? He's setting them free! As a hunter of these plains, I'm finished.

Listen to me, boy. In Uruk lives Gilgamesh. No one—no thing—can beat him. It's a match, god for god or beast on beast—whatever you've got out there, this one's quicker—he moves like a shooting star.

Hie thee to Uruk, I say, and describe this fearsome thing to Gilgamesh.

I'll tell you what he'll say, too. "Trapper, set a trap," he'll say. He'll tell you—sure as a dream I see him:

"Find you a priestess"—you know the ones—those temple courtesans—"Find you a priestess with hearty haunches, and lead her to his haunts...

...and when he should see but himself at waterhole, then let him see her instead, undressing in the bush. Let him see her all. He'll approach—he'll mount her, but at that, his wild friends the animals will have done. They won't go near him then.

Not long, not long before young hunter told his tale to Gilgamesh:
Sir, he must come down from the hills, his strength is unmatched. He moves like a shooting star! He grazes with gazelle, shares with them their watering holes. I dare not approach him. He's filled in my pits, scattered my traps, sets free my measly catch. It is impossible to hunt.

Three days they journeyed, straight for the waterhole, and waited there, as in a hunter's blind—one day, two days waiting, and then late that second day, or maybe the third, the tawny herd moved slowly in to drink.

Yawn

And then he caught himself, thinking of *then*, and thinking of *now*, and thus did he begin with understanding.

He returned and sat himself at Shamhat's feet. He gazed up at her, as if to say, Tell me priestess, fill my head now as you have my loins. And she, pleased with things so far, told him he was wise.

Enkidu, this is understanding now, no different from the gods. Why then run with deer, on the open empty grasslands? Let me take you to Uruk, inside its mighty walls, inside its sacred temple—the goddess whose votary I am, lives there, Ishtar, goddess of love, and her reigning father Anu. And one Gilgamesh, a man as strong as any ox, but like a surly ox, bulls it badly over all his people.

And even as she spoke Enkidu could see a plan, and it pleased him. He liked these magic dancing words; he would have a friend to swap them with.

Up, priestess. Take me to your Uruk, your temple gods, your bully Gilgamesh. Big and bad as he may be, I'll stand up to him.

I will stand in the midst of Uruk and yell out: "I, Enkidu, am the Strongest! Yes, I, I'm as strong as fate: I can change things. I'm the one, the **he**, born on the steppe, the one who is mighty! Strength is my name!"
Let us go then. Let us show him your face. I'll take you there directly. We'll walk straight through the city, among the hordes of people—their bright clothes, they dress as if every day were holiday, do they in Uruk of the massive walls.

Come, we'll wend our way through festive crowds—they twirl, they dance to pipe and drum. And ah, the women! I tell you their very scent will make you dizzy! Their songbird laughter sings gaiety drowns out the grumbling of old and envious men.

O, Enkidu—with so much more to learn—I will show him to you, one as full of life as you, as strong and no less virile: when you look into his face, you'll know: this one is first, day or night he shines with perfect manliness.

Sungod Shamash favors him. And Anu, Enlil and Ea—they all push the borders of his mind: even before we descend these hills, my hairy hulking friend, this Gilgamesh will have a vivid dream of you.

And so it was, as Shamhat saw, great Gilgamesh yawning where he lay, calling to his mother.
What a dream I saw, O, my mother!

And Ninsun, the goddess mother of Gilgamesh, as wise in dreams as everything, said to her son:

This star, too heavy to lift, nonetheless removed to my feet, to receive my blessing as if it were a bride—a bride indeed I see, a companion for my son, born out on the steppe, raised in the wild, as strong and fast as Anu's shooting star: he will help you, son, even as a faithful wife ever by your side. This dream–I tell you it is good, and you will love this friend as never have you loved before.

Mother, wait, I saw another dream. A lot like the first. A lovely axe lay in the temple courtyard, with everyone around it, all of Uruk there. I laid it at your feet. Only this time, I was kissing it, holding it as over a woman, and you....

...you acknowledged it the same as you would me, your son—as equal.

It is the same man. I acknowledged him, and that you love him, a trusty axe: he is loyal, strong, he will be there always when you're in need. An axe, a shooting star...

Meanwhile...
These are images of you, Oh, royal axe! Oh, massive burning star..

—no more was said, for Enkidu did close her mouth with eager loving.
MMM!
SMAK!
SLORP!
SWOON!

Shamhat grew tired of repetitions, both his **flattering her and his flattening her.**
This is a shepherd's bed! Let me up. Get off this ground.

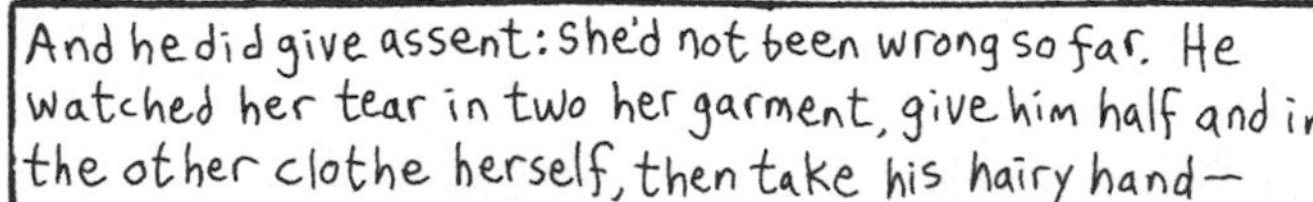
And he did give assent: She'd not been wrong so far. He watched her tear in two her garment, give him half and in the other clothe herself, then take his hairy hand—

Here, put that thing away.

She led him gently as a child to the sheepfold, amidst the shepherds' huts.

The shepherds were amazed, put bread before him, when he'd been used to teats. Warm jets of milk from beneath the bellies of his muzzy kine: what knew he of bread?
?

He gawked, he gagged.
AH HA HA
HA-HA!
HA-HA!
Bleeaghh!
HA
HAH!
HA!

Eat the food, Enkidu. It's on this we live. Here, wash it down with local beer.

And so he chewed, and drank, seven jugs of beer he guzzled, the strong brown beer of Shuruppak fame—he began to sing!
He giggled, his face went flush, he itched all over and rubbed his body down with oil. In short, most human he became.

He took up a weapon, though drunk, and set out to capture lions.
Here Kitty Kitty!

A jackal he caught instead, but the shepherds slept that much better.
You be our watchman, Enkidu the bold! The lion's bane!
HA-HA-HA!! HA!
AHAHA!

And that he was, singing at the edge of camp, nodding at the edge of camp—
ZZZ
SNORT
BZONK!

"Hark! Who's this?!" A man crossed through the pens.
Huh? Whazzat?! Shamhat, bring me that man!
TRUDGE
CRAK!

Why was he there, what was his name? Shamhat hailed the stranger.
Wayfarer, where are you hurrying? You look a mess!
Grrrr.

At Enkidu he spewed his words:
To the meeting house! We're cursed!

This holy place, for sacred marriage—he defiles it with lust. He plays the drum—his own tune!

He calls them to marriage, then steps ahead of the groom. All fair brides—his deflowering! Him first, him, our king! I'm the husband here, yet I'm the next in line!

And all this has been decreed! By gods! At birth, when they cut his cord, it was his lot—They should have cut his cock!

Enkidu went pale, as white as wool. He said naught. He strode out, Shamhat fairly running after him, five stuttered steps to his every one.
Hey, Wait up!

And so he entered Uruk, its busy hum of man, its wide and crowded market place—

The people stared, gathered round and pointed.
He looks just like Gilgamesh!
No, he's shorter.
But the bones are bigger. He's got to be as strong. Maybe...

And some heard tell he's wild, nursed on wild milk; and some rejoiced:
This may be the answer to our handsome randy king!

But some said:
This may be worse— I see a crash of arms ahead.

We'll soon find out. Look where Gilgamesh approaches. Ishtar's made his bed— who's the lucky bride tonight?
WISK SKRITCH
SWEEP SWEEP

But Enkidu raised one foot and blocked the entranceway.
The nuptial chamber was suddenly closed—a thigh as thick as cedar trunk barred Gilgamesh's way.

He grabbed the wild man—
GGNNNAAARRR!!!
YEEAUGHHH!!

SWHOP!
KLONK!
OW!

CKTCH!!
GRRRRR!
!!
LUNGE!

—they fell into the street—
WHUD!
AARRRGH
FWIP!
BOFF!
SKFF

WHOOAH!
SWUT!
HUP!
FLIP

GOOOMPH!
SKRRUNCH!!

KREEGAH! BUNDULO!!
LEAP!

SMASH!
CRAK!
SWOOP!
KERRUNCH!
PLINK!

???
GRNTCH!
TWEET TWEET
HA!

GAHOOUGHRR!!

WHOOMP!
BKRASH!!

—Look! Massive arms locked like horns of bulls. They crashed from wall to wall—the people scattered—
GRRNNYYAUGhhrr!!!
OOOF!
FWWUNCH!
SKRAP!
CLATTER

GRUNT!
Scuffle!!
SPLT

—the door posts split,
KARAAAAK!
HI-YAH!
THWUNK!

AAARRRGH!
GAAAAHH!

sweat and spittle flew—
FFWAPP!

They roared—they crashed—dogs fled—the very walls of Uruk shook!

RUMBLE!!
SHAKE!
THUD!
GGNAARGH!!
WWRROOAHR!!
CRASH!
CRASK!

Slowly the greater brought the lesser to his knee, and, foot on his neck, he turned aside to let his wrath abate.

Enkidu looked at him...

What then? The story blurs. Think of many voices run together, a whirlwind of words. Gilgamesh, panting, but standing tall above the mess they'd made, praised Enkidu to all:
This man hath no equal! This shaggy man, born in the desert...

While Gilgamesh's mother whispered to her serving lady:
Rishat, this Enkidu, he has no mother, no one to cut his hair.
FWT!
SWUF!

He was raised ..by no one!

And Enkidu, looking about for Shamhat, hearing his name praised, and pitied, discovered his cheeks were wet.

His eyes stung, and his strength—it seemed to slip away.
Wwaughh! SOB!

Gilgamesh looked down and saw his tears.
Why the heavy heart, my friend?
BLUBBER!
SNIF!

And Enkidu: Was this what meant 'alone'?
Gilgamesh, you have bested me, hemmed in my strength,

B-bu-but what did you do with it?

My arms still lack their power. My strength keeps flowing out of me, like these woman's tears!
GUSH!
DRIP!
SPLOIK!

Gilgamesh took his hand, pulled him up and embraced him.

Kissed both cheeks, and kissed again, called him brother. Friend.
MMWAH!
SMEK!

Enkidu, I have a plan for us. Far from here to the east lies a great cedar forest. But it has a guardian, one Humbaba, an evil sort set there by Enlil to protect the trees. He is fierce, he is huge- I say let's cut him down, and then his towering trees...

Enkidu stopped him.
My friend, I've been there. When I roamed with kine, I ranged far across hill and plain. From the edge of that very forest, two hours and more into its densest part — there lives, indeed, a monster.

Tall almost as any cedar, he roars like a cataract.

You cannot see his mouth — it's all of flame. His face, a squirming mess. His very breath is death!

You are afraid? I myself am but determined.

Think you of the outcome, the fame, the wealthy wood.
He never sleeps, my friend. One footstep on the path, and he, one full league away, does grumble...

"Hmmm, who treads in my woods? Him will I make faint, him shall I grind to food for my trees." Believe me, King, you won't best him, not Humbaba.

Oh, Enkidu, whose days among us are not numbered?

I will tell you: Only the gods.

You and I will go down; they live on with Shamash. They take Forever as a day. Our great works – are but as the wind.

And here we are still in Uruk and you tell me of fear. How did you stand against me? What lion gladly bared his shaggy throat to your massive hands? Where is Enkidu?
NUDGE!
NUDGE!

Enkidu was silent.
I'll tell you what: I'll go first, you cheer me on behind: "Forward," you say. "fear not." And, even if I fail, what won't they say hence?

"Gilgamesh! He who went down in battle with Humbaba!" Is this not so? "Humbaba the Terrible, Humbaba the Fierce!" Why, crawling up on laps to hear it told, my children's children's children...

Gilgamesh! Enlil put him there on purpose. God's purpose.

Enkidu, you and I, we are young: we have everything to lose.

They poured the molds, monstrous axes did they cast, three talents each.

Not bad.

The people gathered, so too the Elders of the City, and took their seats before him.
Hear me, O Elders of Uruk, I propose to go against the fierce one, Humbaba of the Cedar Forest, and when he hears I'm coming, he will take note.

"Ah, let's see this Gilgamesh," he'll say. "This great scion of Uruk, come to fell my trees. Him I will crush. In Uruk they will feel the land shake beneath their feet."

Indeed, O Elders, it will shake, but with great Humbaba's tumbling. In this I am determined: Such is the everlasting fame I will bring to URUK!!

And there in the crowded marketplace, the Elders all spoke at once...
Gilgamesh! Thou art a pup! So young, your heart much bigger than your head!
You have no idea! His face alone, it wetly writhes like coiled intestines!
This Humbaba changes shapes, it's said. Some say direction!
And would you fight before and aft?
HMph!
That's why he takes his Enkidu, thou dolt!

Though Enkidu was hardly keen...
...to die two hours deep in swaying cedars.

His roar's a whirlwind...
VOOOSHH
WOOAUU!
GAHH!
AROOOOOAAHH!!!!
WHOAA!
CRUMBLE
CRASH!

His jaws are flame...
SKORTCH!
CRACK!
SIZZLE!
POP!

His very breath is death.
WWHOOOSHH!!
PSSSSSS!
choke.
MELT!
DRIP

"Even with your Enkidu, the one is greater than the two." So it went, and Gilgamesh did listen... or pretended to.

In truth, he glanced toward Enkidu and winked.

Then he drew him aside. They spoke so none could hear.
The Elders, too, busily conferred.

Next thing you knew...
May God protect thee, Gilgamesh...
..On the road and all the way back to Uruk's ramparts..
..May you~

And Gilgamesh fell to his knees and prostrated himself.
It is as they say, O Shamash!

God of Justice, to thee I raise my hands, that my life be spared, that within thy Holy Light I return to Uruk's ramparts.
And Shamash spoke...

It wasn't good.

The omens bode...
GLITCH!

..Disaster!
SPLUP!

Yet the Elders brought forth the weapons. Tears did streak our heroes' cheeks...
SNIF

And so they expressed their fears, great strategists all:

Ninsun listened to her son. She rose and withdrew to her inner chamber.

She bathed, she donned her sacred robes and adorned her breast...

...Placed a crown upon her head and climbed the stairway to the roof.

To Shamash she sent thick, smokey incense and raised her arms in prayer.

Why, Sun, didst thou instill this itch for deeds in my only son? Now again you've touched him and he's off - a far distant journey, a road that none has traveled, a fight that's ne'er been fought, yet Gilgamesh sets out to conquer fierce Humbaba, an evil thing that you yourself do hate.

Until that day, O Shamash, from setting out to coming home, from felling cedars to bringing down the evil one, be thou beside him through each of thy days.

I charge you by your own kin, your bright-eyed bride Aia, let her be thy remembrance! And when the sun goes underground, let the watchman of the night stand in!

Then Ninsun snuffed out the incense and summoned Enkidu.
PLNK!

You are not of my womb, mighty Enkidu, and yet I herewith make you so.
POING!

I adopt you. Furthermore, with this necklace, I induct you.

These priestesses you see, these votaries and novitiates...

One among them shall be your wife. Choose now and remember, all your brood shall rank as *you* — as Gilgamesh's brother.
Enkidu stood abashed. A married man, a holy man, charged with his brother's safe return.

Still, to Gilgamesh he whispered low his earlier forebodings.
Turn back, brother. I know this journey's not for you. It's not for anyone.

Then Gilgamesh addressed the mountain.

Up it he climbed, and to it he said, sprinkling about the fine-milled flour:

O Mountain, send me a dream that will gladden my eye!

GLUPH!

FLOOF!

Thereupon a djinn of dust whirled by, sweeping the meal to a perfect circle.

FFWEEEEOOOOOSHHHH!!

WHOOOO!

BLOW!

PUFF!

SWUP!

Thick sleep oozed forth from night, crept up and took him in her arms...

Then dropped him hard in the middle of the watch. Bolting upright, he cried out.
Friend, you called? You must have, You woke me!

That wasn't you, that shook my arm? What disturbed me then?
Huh?

A god passed by? Why else would I feel so drained? Unless it was my dream. No good dream at that.

Enkidu, the whole mountain fell, crumbled down around us and there we perched, puny as two flies of the canebreaks.

I know the canebreaks, I know the open country and its swampy bourn. This dream of yours is most favorable, it has much meaning. Trust me, I know how to read them!

The mountain is of course Humbaba. The flies, if you'll forgive me, are you and I. We shall seize him!

We shall bring him crashing to our feet. We'll sit, like flies on the rubble heap of his enormous corpse. Shamash will tell you this at dawn.

Enkidu, when the heavens roar, when the earth roars back. When the day turns night and in the lightning flash one sees a rain of death, then it's time, my friend, even as this dream's fire fades to embers then to smouldering ash, it's time we descend this mountain. Seek advice in lower climes. This is my final dream.

On, and on again, they lunged up the slope, through woods until...

The Gate!

They stood before it, dumb. Dazed, they gazed on the other side– at wide paths where Humbaba trod!

The shade was deep: the trees immense, they craned their necks – all was cool and quiet, and pungent with cedar scent. Yet, was that a watchman making off, through the brambled underbrush?

Enkidu addressed the gate.
Oh thou gate, be thee dumb but comely. From forty leagues I saw your shining timber, even before the towering cedars, and behold thy lock and bolt, and this old-fashioned pivot – I think nothing in Nippur compares!

So grand was this gate that Enkidu put down his axe to firmly grasp the handle..

WWONK!
...And as quick, his hand turned wholly numb!

My hand! It's crushed! Gilgamesh, my friend, my hand feels but a stubby wrist – we can't go on, I'm crippled!
THROB
PULSE!
ACHE!

Enkidu, was it not you reminding me of Uruk's square, my lofty boasting there, within these last two hours? Now you would turn back, after our travail? You who've fought your battles surpassing well, you no stranger to this place, you suddenly a coward?
SNIFF!

Give me this palsied hand: place it here on my heart. Dismiss death and think of fame, whatever it may cost. Think life, Enkidu. Guard thine with all thy might so you may guard mine, as I ever yours – together now we will burn with conquest.

And they entered the cedar forest. All was quiet as a dream.

Stark still they stood, in awe, before the green and towering grandeur. Above, the cedars touched the sky.

Drop down—The matted paths where monster stalked, as wide as avenues.
After you!
Tracking would be easy.

Cast gaze out upon the mountain, reminder of whose sometime throne this was, Ishtar in her most ferocious guise: Irnini.

One cedar, perhaps the father here, raised its teeming arms as if to bless the mountain. In its shade they felt a thrill, a happiness, while scent of cedar singed like holy incense.

Without a word Gilgamesh picked up the axe, swung hard. Chips flew like a startled forest bevvy—or bright sparks. (His mountain dream?)
HYAH!
HACK!
CHOP!
BOING!
KERCHUNK
His neck, his back: thick ropes of working muscle.

Not long before the crashing of that stately, falling tree... kept right on crashing, became a ringing voice...
Who defiles my wood?! Who's that hacking at my mountain's cedars?
BKRRUNNCHH!!
SNAP!
KREEE KRAK KUH BWOOM
And another voice—rumbling on the air....
Advance, Gilgamesh Be not afraid!!

A bird announced their presence...
BRIP

Another answered—soon a Piping, chirping tumult.
ICKA ICKA
BRIP?

Crickets joined the chorus.
CHUUURRRR
CHIRRiiiP

A pigeon moaned, a dove cooed back,
The monkeys chattered like women at a well.
EEEP
COOOO
CHRT
YIP YIP
KRRR
WHOOK
PEEP
Aiee
PIP
HWAA
KAW
YA
BRAAP
FWT
POK
ZZZZ
POK
QUALP
GOOMPH
WONK
HISS

A baby monkey shrieked!
YEEEEK

This was Humbaba's entertainment: an orchestra of din.
KREEEEEEEE
OOOK
Yiii
!!
YOWL
ZZT
AHROOGAH
HEEYAW
OOK
HONK
YAP
PRRPP
TWEET
GRiii
ARF
PLOP
GRiii
GRAAUGH
HUUUiii
FRFPH
BRAK
ZiNG
CROAK
DitDit DitDit
MOOO
!!

Thereupon, great Gilgamesh lay himself down and promptly fell asleep!
PLONK!
ZZZZZ

Or so it seemed. Unable to get up, he saw swords, spines of light, he saw bright sheaths and daggers in a whirl. He saw them glow like light.
BZZZMMM! Fwiip!!
KZZIIING!!
Schwuushhh!
ZIP!
VVVVWEEEOOOO!!!
VUT!
PTHFWT!!

His own axe grew verdigris, streaked with rust. Enkidu shook him hard:
Gilgamesh, this is the way home prone, on a bier! Arise!!

He saw Humbaba's face: he thought he'd become an augur staring entrails down.
PLIP!
BLUP!
SPLURT!

He saw himself do battle with the weapons made from light; he chased them...
ZZZZ
FWEEOOP!!
VOOOOOEEEOOO!
FWT
ZIP!!
VVWIP!
BBZWONT!!

Let them go! They are but the chicks! The hen, the hen! Get the hen, we'll crush the fledglings later!
DONK!

The awful voice, the fiery breath behind it:
Hum, So! Have we here now: the madman and the ape in consultation? If it's advice you seek - is it "Bilgamesh"? - be sure to ask this hairball why you're here. This Enkidu, this son of a fish - without a father even...
... You're both so puny I think I see a turtle, not the sort to suck its mother's milk - so I step over.
...Which he did!

Then Humbaba plucked them from the ground.
But even if I squashed you both – it's not a filling meal!! Ah-haha Haaaughh!
SWIPE!
YOINK!

En-ki-duuu! Enkidu, I tremble!
TWIT! TWEET! TWEET!

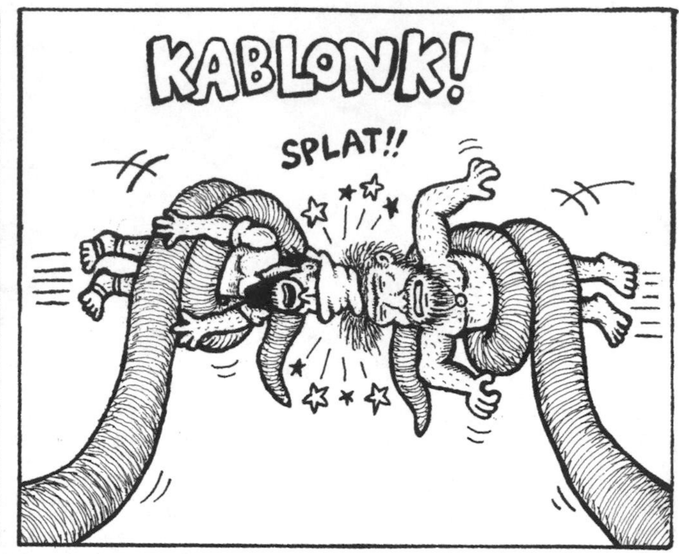
KABLONK!
SPLAT!!

BOM! BOUM! BOM!
Two are stronger!

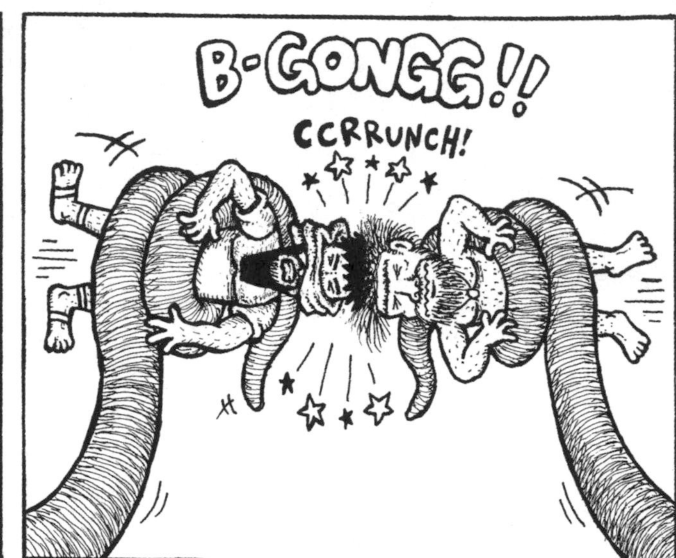
B-GONGG!!
CCRRUNCH!

Ulp...
Two cubs can turn the lion!!

PFFWOP!!
SMACK!

He swung them in the air.

I'll bite clean through this neck!!

Enkidu, old fur frog, why did you lead him to me?

Call on your weapons now, my friend, call them by their names!

SLORP!

GAK!

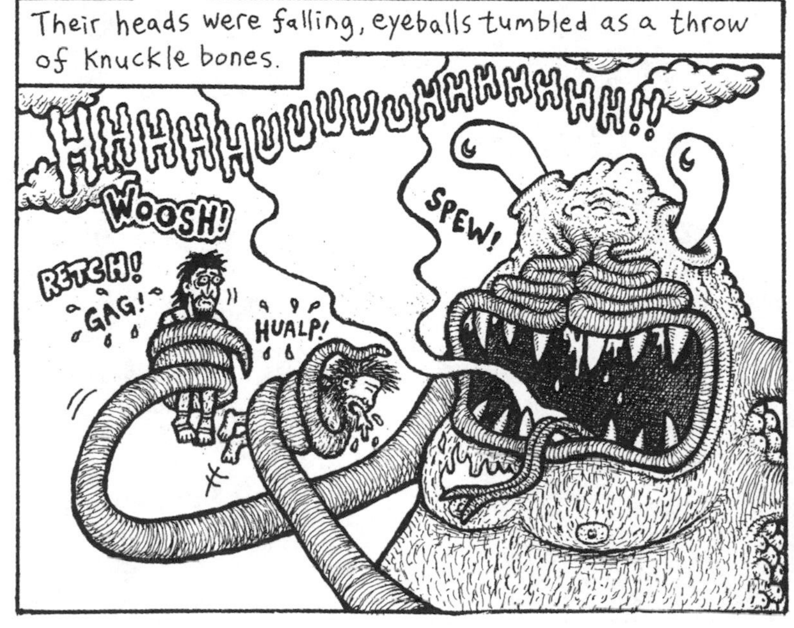

Beat and split it with their feet! New gorges for the mountains, billows for the sky, stirred up, carved out, by the heels of heroes' feet.
BASH!
BONK!
POW!
THUD!
WHAM!
KRAK!
SLAM!

The clouds went black, the fog wrapped round like death.
WHACK!
BAM!
THWOP!

Through his streaming tears Gilgamesh prayed to Shamash.
Glorious one, back in Uruk we divined a path. Have I not followed it?

Was this to be its end?!
SMUSH!

And Shamash, heavenly Shamash, did hear...

...So weighty winds rose up.

Mighty winds began to rush and howl: the North, the South,

HAADWOOOOOOOOLLLL!

SLIP!

FFWUUUUUUSHHHH!

Humbaba's gaping mouth- No roar, no flame- the winds did steal his breath.

FFFWiiiiiiiiiUUU!
WHHHOOOOOOOOOOOOOOOOSHHHH!!
STAB!
SQUIK!
HACK!
SPUTTER!
GUSH!
FWT!
CHUNK!

Schweeeeeoooooooeeee!!!
YARGH!
GLIK!
ZING!
TRIP!
BLUP
THUK!
KABOOOOM!
SPLAT!

Humbaba, who'd planted every tree that swayed here—Gilgamesh, young and gold, a goddess' son, scion of Uruk, favorite of Shamash—gasping, Humbaba said...
Offspring of gods, darling of the sun—who has had a hand in this, I see—I can make you master here, master of these trees. I'll keep them for you, harvest them and build your palace, all of fragrant myrtle. You are the King, full master now, and I am your willing servant... ...Just let me go!
SKWT!
ZIP!
STOMP!
FLOP!

Enkidu, above the winds, made himself be heard.
Gilgamesh, don't listen to this ogre!
FWWiiiSHH!
BLURP!
SPOIT!
HUUUWAAAA
THUD
Ach- I should have fed you to the eagles...
WAAAAA!
... stomped you out at the gate, before any leaf of mine had touched your face! Thou mite! Thou hired hand, slave who yeses master and yeses yet again!
SQUISH!

Enkidu, hot in Gilgamesh's ear:
Kill him! Grind him into paste!!
Parasite, you know Enlil's rules, you know his pact. Only for this moment have you any power: Use it wisely, mortal. Be clement: tell Gilgamesh to Spare my life!

Do it while the Gods are turned away, before Enlil can hear —
GOOOMPH!
BOOT!

— they'll object, but we'll erect a monument to this feat, how Gilgamesh slew the evil of the forest. I tell you, friend: He must not live!!

At which Humbaba cries a curse:
None here shall grow old then! And may the lot of Enkidu be Shorter even than his friend's!!!
KWWWUUUUUU
CHOP!
Gilgamesh did hesitate, and Enkidu did yell:
Heed me! Listen to thy friend, Gilgamesh! Not this monstrous forest sentry, this unholy face of guts!
WHAK
GLUG!
GLOOP!
FWAP!

With that, the axe swung down, deep in Humbaba's neck...
SPLERTCH!
PHWK!
Blood gushed, men hacked hard, cut out his cursing tongue, pulled forth his entrails like hauling ropes of river barges.
CHOP!
GLK!
HACK!
SWOOP!
SLASH!
GURGLE!
RIIP!
FLAP!
FWUP! FWP
GNAR!
GLUB! BLUB!
Abundantly the guts did spill down the mountain's slippery slope.
Still they cut the cedars. Gilgamesh chopped the trees. Enkidu pulled at stumps. They paused.
Friend, here's one to behold. It used to scrape the sky. Let's make a door of it, twice twelve cubits wide, three times that in height. The post alone, one cubit, and hinges from a single piece. We'll carry it downriver to Nippur on a raft.
CHOP! HACK! SLASH!

A cedar raft they strapped together, and set out, Euphrates borne. Enkidu worked the oar...
SPLUP!
SPLASH!
GRAAAK!
SNAP!
GLOOSH!
FLOIT!
...While Gilgamesh hoist-ed high, and held aloft
HUMBABA'S GORY HEAD!!!

Back in Uruk now, they purify their bodies. Gilgamesh is washing his clotted hair, scraping gore from weapons.
SPLISH SPLASH!
PLOOOOSH!
RUB A DUB!
GLUG!
FWUSH!
PLIP!
SPLUB!
PLOIK!
BLUP!
FWAP

He shakes loose his locks; they slap upon his back.
FLUP!
KA-THWAK

Throws off his filthy clothes and dons fresh-smelling robes.
SNIP! CLIP! SNIP!

Snaps on armlets, cinches tight his sash,
SPROUT
POING!

and, regal now, his crown he settles on his head.

This goes not unnoticed. The goddess Ishtar lifts up her eyes at beauteous Gilgamesh.
Gilgamesh, come, be my love. This fruit of your body, give it to me as a gift. Even be my husband, even call me wife. A chariot I'll fit thee with, of lazuli and gold, golden wheels, and hubs of precious stone. The mules you hitch to — demons from a storm!
ZZAAP

Gilgamesh was silent. Ishtar went on:
You'll enter our house through fumes of cedar. Servants and priests, lower than the threshold and dais will they bow down to kiss thy feet.
Kings, too, bowing before thee. Princes, lords and rulers—all will scrape, bringing thee as tribute the yield of mountains and plains.
Hear me, Gilgamesh, thy goats—they shall drop triplets, thy sheep twins. Thy stallion, famed abroad for its gallop; thy mules in harness—no other chariot come near.

Gilgamesh opened his mouth:
Great Lady, what, pray, shall I give thee, an I become thy husband?

Oil, yes, for thy lovely body; divine robes, too. Do you eat bread? Must I bake bread fit for a god?

Wine, whose vineyards lie in heaven—am I tall enough? Where is my advantage here?

Taking you in marriage is like moving into rooms without a roof. You're but a flapping back door against the stinging wind. You're a turban slipping down over the eyes, a bottle that dribbles on its carrier, pitch that besmears the bearer, a gaping pit that swallows its digger, the elephant that will shrug off its blanket, and will again. Goddess, you are limestone that crumbles deep in the bowels of a rampart.
BUMP
WWHOOOOSSHHH!!!
PWUFF
KLAKKETY KLAK!
BONK!
BONK
SPLAT
SMUSH!
SQUICH!

Like a glorious palace of knights that crashes to pieces on everyone's head—
O, thou sandal that bites the foot...
Do tell, lady, which husband of thine was it that thou didst love for ever?

Say, which little shepherd of thine, O, star of morning, star of evening, could keep thee in contentment, for even a tiny part of ever??
Harken, goddess, I can answer. For you I shall recite your list of ruined lovers:

Your first, Tammuz, shepherd of Uruk, yearly we mourn his death; each year at spring we see him brought back from the Underworld-his year-long tears, your decree.

And the gay-feathered roller bird you loved, and did smite him, so he flies ever on a broken wing, looping and rolling, or merely stands in the grove: "Kappi, kappi, my wing, my wing!"
WAAUGHHK! KAPPI-KAPPI!
Kappi-kappi?

Wasn't there a lion, a mighty magnificent lion, whose pit you dug, seven on seven deep?
WHOOARRRARAW!!!
FWUNCH!
SNAP!

"A stallion, I think, unmatched in battle, you honored with whip and spur, drove him to seven on seven leagues at full gallop, to refresh himself up to his wearied withers, in the muddy murk of the water where he stood."
GASP!
HUFF
WHAKOW!
SPLERCH
GLOP!
PLUFF!
"His mother, Silili, weeps for him still."

"And there among the shepherds, was that their leader, who slaughtered his kids each day for you?"
Phew!
GAAK!

"Who endlessly heaped up the ash-cakes, warm and golden, for you?"

"And you clouted him good, turned him into a jackal,"
KAZOINK
BZZAP!
!?

"So his own herd boys drove him off, and his dogs tore at the backs of his legs!"
WROARHFFF!!
YAP
AWROOO!
YIP
CHOMP!
GNAARR!!

"Ishullanu, your father's gardener, you loved passing well, for keeping you in flowers and succulent dates."

That one caught your eye. "O, Ishullanu, come to me, my love. It's time to taste your manhood. Give me your hand and touch here my slit, cleft like your dates of the willowy palm."

I have food aplenty, goddess. I want not. My mother bakes for me. Should I nibble then at wickedness?

My grass coat keeps me warm enough.

"You took it well..."

"One fillip on his noggin and he became a bug!"
BZZWONT!
ZORT!
?!

Stuck there in between: can't go up the rushing drainspout..."
BLUP
Uh oh...
FLOOSH

"...and the buckets bash below."
DRIP!
SPLISH SPLASH
OOOOF!
BLOOP!

And I should step in line, eh? You'd love me as reverently as all of them?
Ishtar heard:

her fury blasted her straight up to heaven.
FATHER!!!

To Anu she cried, and to her mother Antu she went weeping.
O, father, insult upon insult has he heaped on me, rubbing my nose in naughtiness, my venal sins, my several indiscretions.
Quite, and did you ask as much? Did you not bid for Gilgamesh's manhood? Your "indiscretions," daughter, are a thing a fellow would be wise to think about – it's a heavy, loathesome dowry you bring!

Father dear. Do this or else: Lend me the heavenly bull, let it descend on Uruk, nostrils all aflame, and let Gilgamesh be gored on holy horns!

Anu stared at her and rubbed his brow. Ishtar went up close:
If you do not give me this Bull of Heaven, I will smash the Gate of the Underworld, I will crush its bolt so the door swings open, and you will have the legions of the dusty dead sitting down to dinner with the living.
Yeow!
No! Grandma-Don't! Aughh!
Aiee!

Ishtar, if you demand this bull from me, famine will follow. Seven years of sun-baked husks, dry as parchment. Have you gathered grain, or fodder for the cattle?
CLAP! CLAP!

Of course! I have heaped the corn in granaries, I've grown the grass for kine. None will bite the dust of empty husks! Much grain I've collected for the people, much grass for animals have I grown.

Anu, hearing this, but placed a rope into her hand.
PAT PAT
?
It went taut:
POING!
!!!
through black and huffing nostrils it looped, round nose of monstrous bull.
THE BULL OF HEAVEN!!
KBZZZZVVRRRREEEEEEEEEEEEOOOOOOOOSHHHHHH
– happily she led it down to Uruk.

It stopped at the river, where it was seen.
Many men and seven closed in upon it.
It snorted once, blasting out a pit: a hundred men fell in.
GGRRROOONNKAK
KNA-BOOOOOMM!!
KLONK
It snorted twice,
SNOOOORRRKK!
GNERT
Chuff
...and twice one hundred men of Uruk, and then another hundred, fell into the gaping pit.
PFA-DOOOOM!!!
AAHWWHOOOGAAHHH!!
CHARGE!! oh well, never mind...
DOOONT!
TROMP
SMUSH!
THUD!

A third time, Enkidu fell in up to his waist.
yeeuck!!
WAWOOOOOOOOORF!
GGRRRRRRR!!
SCRUFF!
SKRFF!
He leaped out and grabbed at the Bull.
YEEAARRGGHH!!
WRHOOOWAUGHH!!
BOING!
SKRUNK!

Its slippery horns, its frothing mouth,
Whoops!
SSLIP
RUMBLE! RUMBLE!
CLOPPITY CLOP
KA-POW!!
its lashing tail—
LASH!
ZÏNG!!
SCRAMBLE
did spray them all with dung!
KA-BLOOOOK!!!
Guh-SPLATCH
FFWUUUP!!!
SPLERT
PLOOOPHFFF!
GWAP!

mmMOOOOOWRONK!!
Gilgamesh! I've got his horns! Aim for the nape!
SPROING
GALUMPH! GALOOMPH!
RUMBLE!! THUD!

ZZLOOOP!!
YOINK!
ERT
SSKREEEE

RRRIP!!
CRUNCH!
GORE!! GORE!
SKRAATCH

They went round...
GRAAHGOOAHH!
MULCH!!
SLASH!
UNGH!!
SSKKRAAPE!!

...and then...
WWHiiiP!
Only by his tail! Beware his slashing horns!!
SNORT!

Somehow, between the nape of neck and dragged-down head, with Enkidu tossed all about, Gilgamesh plunged home!
FLU-CHUK!
SNWOOOP

A butcher could not, on a carcass still free of flies, a cleaner cut effect.
WOBBLE
GLUK
BLUP!
PLIP

They struck it down,
KA-FLUMP!
GUSH!
BOING!
SQUIK

and, having done so, straightaway removed its innards.
FLURP
SPLORTCH!
GLOOP

And then they sat down together, two brothers: this was work well done.

Ishtar climbed up the rampart...

High on the wall, she crouched in ritual lamentation. In rage she cursed the hero:
This Gilgamesh, reviling me with Slanders, now has killed the Bull of Heaven. Woe on him who besmirches me! Woe to them that slay the bull!!
Enkidu listened to her Shrieking wail, rose up,

tore off the bull's right thigh,
RRRRIPP!
SNAP!
CRACKLE!
POP!

and hurled it in her face!
?
FWUP!
HEAVE

KBLONK!
SPLAT!
zzzzzWIP!
OW!
If I could catch, you Goddess, I'd treat you just the same! I'd strap entrails around your neck— a lovely, bloody choker!

Ishtar- having enough of that-quietly called her women, the priestesses and the sacred courtesans
and over the bloody thigh she she led forboding lamentations.

For his part, Gilgamesh called out the masters of the crafts—
the artists, the armorers, all the artisans he called, to see the span of horns,
azure horns of lapis lazuli, thirty pounds apiece as each was wrapped two fingers thick; each when hollowed bore oil in sixty gallon jugs.

This ointment he presented to Lugalbanda, his tutelary god, anointing his image that very night.
GLUB

And into that quiet room he carried the horns, hung them on the walls of the holy family place, abode of all his ancestors.

The people crowded the streets to see them. The men, the women, the singers and dancers closed in beside them – Gilgamesh leaned down and asked:

Who's the giant now? Who are the bull fighters, which is your hero most splendid?

Among men, he's the finest, they said – the women thought so, too. Even if Ishtar's angry, who else among men could please her?

Gilgamesh, Gilgamesh... The chanting went on through the night,
GIL-GA-MESH! GIL-GA-MESH!

the revels ran late in the night.
CRASH!

In the palace, one and then another, man and then woman and then man—one by one,

all fell fast asleep,
SNORK!
SPLASH
PSSSSS!
Ahhhh!

while visions stalked the halls,
and Enkidu saw his.

He moaned out to his friend:
Why.... Why the great gods—all gathered in a meeting?
Huh? Wha-?

And day returned. Enkidu called out to Gilgamesh.
Hear me, hear what dream I saw last night...

It was Anu and Enlil, it was Ea, and heavenly Shamash, too-all of them, all in counsel together...

"Anu was nodding his head at Enlil and saying "because.'"

Because they have killed the Bull of Heaven, and because they have killed Humbaba, one of them must die.

Now which one stripped the cedars?

But Enlil interrupted...
Enkidu shall die! Gilgamesh shall not!

Then Shamash said to Enlil...
Humbaba and the Bull of Heaven, both at whose request? You cannot kill them innocent. One urged, the other struck, and I was there in spirit.

Enlil was enraged and snapped at my sun Shamash...
You were there in whirling winds! Every day, you go down to them, like comrades who eat salt together!

Enkidu took ill, lay there tossing on his bed. Gilgamesh knelt beside him weeping, tears pouring from his eyes like beads from Enkidu's hot brow.
Brother, dear Brother — Why exonerate me while they put you through this?

He wiped the sopping brow and wrung the cloth, and his thoughts went cold...
Shall I soon be squatting by the spirit of the dead?
Nay, outside the door of the spirit of the dead, never again to see thee?

Enkidu raised up on elbows.
You stupid door! Whose idea were you?
What? Who—me?

My measures we laid out, all your cubits tolled by me! Thy post and pivot, stanchion, lock and socket... No Nippur craftsman could do better!

You tried to lame my hand, and now... Had I known...
FLAP!
FLUP!

Had I but known your beauty to pay me back like this, my axe you would have tasted, the raft I would have made of you!

Enkidu, you're babbling!
I brought you there, I carried you to Nippur, this was my good turn.

But the King who follows me, he goes through, Gilgamesh steps through your portals.

Gilgamesh scrapes off my name. You will speak of Gilgamesh, not Enkidu!

With which he grasped the door and hurled it in the air, all in the air and of the air, a gruesome pantomime.
GURRK!!

O, Enkidu, you whose plans I always made my own, these words come not from thy heart, although... Although I fear the dream is prescient. (Although its sense appalls.)
FUME!
SPUTTER!

Enkidu, good friend. Talk sense. Heart and mind together-this the gods did gift to you, yet speak you now like twenty madmen...
Seventy-two...

Seventy two cubits.

And Gilgamesh concurred with nods, head bowed. Past his tears he could not see...
This dream is good, but you frighten me.
Uuuhggh... ...groan...

Enkidu reached for his face.
Your wood was without compare, comely in mine eyes!
?!
GRAB!
GOINK!

He snatched his hand...
I- I'm no gate!
I am pain. Pain's their gift now, a year of pain, raw legacy of gates and gods.

Gilgamesh leapt up.
Like flies, man! Your lips are buzzing like flies!
No other like you, in my eyes without compare,

Chop you up! Lash your planks into a raft!

I'll go pray! I'll find your private god - is it god or goddess?

I'll send her to horned Anu, or to his son Enlil, great counselor. I'll put your statue there before them. They cannot forget. My golden Enkidu will snare their eye.
ZZZZ!

Enlil we'll bring around. He can't go back - I mean, he can.

I mean, what he has said... the gods can change their minds, you know...

We'll glorify him, honor him to save his face...

He knew better. Enlil, Lord Wind, fixer of destinies, would not take back his verdict.
UNGH!
DROOL!
SOB!
WEEP!
The dream, the gate, the very name of Enkidu that Gilgamesh scraped off in Enkidu's grim dream, Enlil would erase.

The day awoke. First glow of morning and Enkidu's head came up and he began to weep.
The sun filled up the room: it was surely Shamash paying him a visit.
Shamash, listen to my appeal: from the outset, I've been gypped!

"Beginning with that hunter—that scoundrel— because of him I'll not see half of what my friend will have, so let this hunter get his own half measure.

Half enough to eat, half his game escape before his very eyes. Half, I say, and half that half to go. Half his strength, half his profit, half his happy share in life...
And as for the remainder half, let it vanish out the window."

He felt better: it prompted him to curse that temple whore, his tutor Shamhat.

Come, woman, come see your benefits. Hear my curse, and may it become so this minute! Gone your lovely rooms, no more receive young vigor in your loins. Let your lap be lousy, demons pepper it. May you be barren, may the young girls bar your way. May beer slop on your dress; on your robes, the drunk shall heave his vomit.
UNGURK!
HLORF!
GLAP!

"You've seen the last of silver, of alabaster nicknacks. May you walk the streets, give birth in an alley, to an infant quick as used up clay. Your turf — may you ply your trade beneath the shadow of the wall!

Your clients, stumbling drunks, they'll slap you for your pay. It's only just I will you this, for teaching me to shun my friends, deathless on the steppe."

"This Gilgamesh, will he not lay you out on a great dais, a couch of honor?

Your statue, he will set at the left of his throne: all the princes of the world will kiss your graven feet.

Uruk will mourn you past endurance, moaning will replace song in Uruk.
AAAUGHHHH!!

I tell you this is so: When you are gone, Gilgamesh will turn foul. Dirty, sunken, hungry. Filthy matted hair and lion skin is all he'll wear, roaming the open country."

"Two leagues away, they'll be primping, trimming beards, asking servants 'How do I look?' The young soldiers running, loosing girdles as they come.

Lapis and gold, gems incarnadine will shower you! He who would wrong thee, he will pay completely, he will be devastated! Only that he presents you to his household gods, will he not lose all."

Enkidu sunk back then, patted her hand and smiled.
Thou harlot divine, my teacher in flesh and mind, recall you that honored woman, all perfection she, with the seven lovely children? Her husband will abandon her for you.

He slipped back into sleep.
ZZZZZZZZZ

He woke.
?

He called out.
!

No one came.
...

He slept again.
Z

When he awoke, Gilgamesh was there.

They spoke ~ holding nothing back.
In my dream, the heavens moaned and the earth groaned back and I stood there in between. You know what that portends. Then came a seeming youth, his face in shadow, but I glimpsed lion-headed Anzu. He had a lion's paws, with talons of an eagle.

"He seized me by my hair ~ I fought — he was lightning quick, skittered like a top, and strong!
He turned me on my head, a grip I couldn't break ~ I couldn't breathe!

"Help me, friend!" I cried. But you—

—it's but a dream, a fretful dream...

You were afraid, old friend, and did not move to help me.

Wait, there's more.

"Then he made a dove of me — no hands, my arms all feathers, and like a dove he carried me. Arms pinioned to my sides, down we went!

... down to the House of Darkness, which has no exit, no traveler returns, there is no light for them; dust is their sustenance, clay their bread.
Like drab birds, they're draped in feathers— dust coats everything. Off in a corner, I saw a mound of dusty royal crowns; they weren't piled there to be cleaned.

Those ancient rulers, once proud owners of those crowns, serving men now, waiting on Anu and Enlil – here's warm food, sweets, coolest water from the waterskins...

...while for themselves, the House of Dust! High priests of death presiding.

The seer sitting there,

and acolyte; the purifying priest, the madly prophesy-ing one –

all the anointed ones of the greater gods,

...and Etana, King of Kish, carried off by an eagle,

Queen of the Underworld, Ereshkigal, before whom kneels the scribe: she holds up the tablet, and he reads out their fates. She looked up and saw me."
Who brings this one here?!

This is a dream, a dire, awful, forboding dream.
I wish you'd been there...

We always travel together!

Uhh~ heh-heh...
HAR-HAR! Hyuck chortle...
They spoke of their travels, their battles and their scrapes.

Gilgamesh tried to cheer him: – Remember the lions?
You were afraid! I prayed to the moon!
Ha Ha Ha Ha
BWAH HA HAW!
No good dream that night, either... But here we are. Two lions less... You won't forget?

From the day of that dream, Enkidu declined. Two days asleep, not eating. Two more, his flesh the color of the sheets.

Five. Six. Seven days he lingered.

An eighth, a ninth, it worsened still. A tenth. And an eleventh.

Twelve days, Enkidu, in his bed, twelve days he languished ill, then called out to his friend:
You, may you die in battle. This bed is shame. If...

If we were in battle, you would save me now! Even now. You did before, as I you.

My friend is cursing me, thinks Gilgamesh.
All the times I balked—my friend, so strong—he's the one to finish every fight

He, put off **my** shame.

He calls upon me now, again. Me.

He dies because of me.

Enkidu made a terrible noise, like a dove whose throat is cut. It startled Gilgamesh. He began to wail:
AAUGHUUHKKLL Uuhhhh—
O, first among men! O, may he not go down in death! May he not be clamped by...

He stopped, looked down at his friend: "I will mourn him."
"I will be beside you."

TABLET VIII

Dawn stole across the room, clung to things: fluttered like life on Enkidu's face. Gilgamesh talked to the corpse:
You were sired by a wild ass, nursed by gazelle, taught to graze by the herds. Your paths through the pastures—your road up the mountain—the Cedar Forest won't forget thee! May it mourn.

"May the elders of Uruk mourn, and all the people on the streets that reached out for us, shouting out blessings...

...and the men we encountered, in the hills, on the grasslands—

—may these lands themselves echo with shrieks as if they were thy mother."
WWHOOOOOOWLL!

The tiger, the panther, hyena and jackal, cheetah and leopard, bull and ibex and stag—noble heads bowed all, low in the grass.

The river banks where we walked, Ulaya's spangled beauty, quiet for ever, or the pure Euphrates, no other water for your waterskin would you have, shall not these rivers notice? Shall not their waters weep?"

When you went round with the Bull of Heaven, when we struck it down...

Come now, ye elders of Uruk, give ear to me! O, men of Uruk, what you hear is my weeping, keen as the wailing of women!

The axe, it slips in my grip, my bow unstrung; the sword of my belt, the shield before me, my festival clothes, sash of my loins—a demon has fancied them, made off with them all.

And to Enkidu he said,
My younger brother Enkidu. My friend. Swift as a wild ass, sure as a panther, leopard of open country—we met once, we climbed a mountain, we seized the bull. And killed it. Humbaba of the Cedar Forest... we brought him down!

And now? You sleep? You can't shake off a little sleep?

Listen to me! Are you listening? Break open your dark!

But Enkidu could not raise his head. Gilgamesh lay his hand upon the breast. It was still. He gently covered the face, as he would a bride's with a veil.

Then he leapt up—ranged the room, swooped like an eagle, like a lioness robbed of her cubs he paced the room, whirled back and forth—from his throat came the gutteral moan of a lion.
wwHOOAUUUAAGH!!

He tore out his hair, the tufts flew about...
YANK!
Aieeee!
PULL!
TUG!

...ripped off his clothes like they stung him.
GGRRAAH!
REND!
TEAR!
RRiiP!!

Till dawn like this...
YEEARGHH!
SMASH!
THUD
KLUMPH!
BONK

... then shouted out through the door—smiths and jewelers he summoned...
SMITH! JEWELER! Get in here--NOW!
O, copper and silversmiths, O, lapidary! The king will have a statue of his friend.

Alabaster here, lazuli for the chest, his skin shall be all of gold. Thirty minas, at the least! No, thirty here, and here.
His limbs... His sword? Here, use mine, the blade... the handle in lapis lazuli, the haft inlaid with carnelian.

Gilgamesh planned for his statue.

Thy gilded image will rest well, my friend, and recline on a royal couch. It will sit on a comfortable throne at my left— its feet too, will they kiss, the princes and monarchs will pay homage.

And I will take it into the city where Uruk will weep— busy workers, lovely maids and noble men will put aside their lives to mourn you, grief will flood their daily designs, whilst I...

I shall go unkempt.

My hair unshorn, my face bestreaked, wearing only the skin of a lion will I roam the desert plains...

... the steppes that were your home, the barren steppe, where range the restless ghosts.

Silent, in the dawn, Gilgamesh performed a ritual—
—alone dragged out a massive table of Syrian wood, filled with honey a large bowl of carnelian...
... and another of lapis lazuli he filled up with butter. These he adorned and left to the sun, to Shamash, for his approval. Thus did Gilgamesh commend his friend to the gods.

And now he weeps as he walks, ranging across the barren desert. Again, and again he buries his friend, bitterly weeps, rails at this end, then feels it rise in his belly: an iron black thought:
I too shall die. Am I not like him?

It writhed and stuck in his belly:
Someday, like my friend—*my very self!* This I fear as nothing else. It makes me roam this ghastly steppe, cringing over death. My death. So. Bend, then, footsteps! Toward Ubar-Tutu's son. Make haste, I say, to the Faraway, to Utnapishtim, the one alone who's not gone down in dusty death.

Night fell in the mountain passes, and lions shared his way, skulking beside in the dark.

Fear and fear again, he raised his face to pray. To the moon, *Sin*, he prayed, or to any god who'd listen:
Protect Thou me.

Then in his sleep he saw them in a gambol, bloody lion snouts rejoicing.
SPT!
CRACKLE!

He woke enraged—
Huh? What the-?!
SNIFF

RRROARRR!
GRAB!

KRK
WHUD!
FWSSHH!!

OOOWWOOO!!

–grabbed a hatchet, snatched his short sword from its sheath.
Like an arrow he shot into that growling pitch of dark, wheeling and flailing...
YEEAARRGH!!
GRRRRRR!!

...screaming he leaped among them.–
KREEGAH!
BUNDULO!
LEAP
GRR! SNARL!
SPRING

UMPH!
THUD!
HYOWWL!
SKRT

GNARF!
CHOMP!
CLAW!
GRRRR!

GRRAARR!
CHOP!
JAB!
GHUUKH!

Which the lion, which the man all red with gore?
WRAAARR!
GRAAAH!

SLASH!

FWUD!
WOOAGH

EEYARRLL!
UNGH
SKRATCH!

RRROOAARR!!

SNARL!
POKE!
GRAB!

CHOMP!
OW!
FWP!

UUUUURRRGHH!

CHUK!
GARR

WOOOAAAAAAHHHHRR!!
GRUNT!

GROWL!
SNAP!
LUNGE!

GNYAAARRLL!

HHYAAAKKLLLK!
JAB!

When he breathed again, two lions lay there butchered.

They call the mountain Mashu— the Twin Peaks.

The one reaches up to heaven...
FLAP!
SQUAWK!
FLUP!

...the other dives below, like mirrored in a pond.

They stand opposing sentinels at the daily rising of the sun, and the nightly burrowing of the sun.

The nether peak plunges deep, to reach the dreary Underworld, where, sentries at its gates, scurry the **akrabu-amelu**...
CRUMBLE!
SLIP!
POK!
... creatures half man, half scorpion!
TCHAK!
BONK!
?
They beam abroad their terror, and terror shines: it glints off mountain slopes, and their one sharp glance is death.
CHITTER! CHITTER!
At dawn and at dusk, they guard great Shamash of the sun–his going down, his rising.

SKRK!
CHiT!
CHiT!
CHiT!
SKT!
SKRiT!
CHT!

KRK!
BRKLK!
PWFK!
BUMP!
YIIII!
SCRAPE!
SKIIID!
TCHAK!
PKPT!

CLONK!
THUD!
BOP!
WHUK!
PNK!
CHIT! CHT!
CRASH!
CHRT!
OOF!

TOPPLE!
SKREEEEEEEEE!
WUNCH!
SPLT!
SKLK!
SNAP!

YEOW!
SKRAAA!
CHIT!
CHT!
CLACK!

KICK!
FWAP!

KRTCH!
SCHIT!
SKUTTER!

KZAK!
BRKT!
PRT!
DUK!
TAK!
PAK!
POHK!
KAPUK!
SPLIT!

When Gilgamesh saw them closing in, his face went dark with gloom.

He shook, and could not speak, but he approached...

CHITTER!
CHT!

He bowed down before their leader, who said, calling to his wife:

It's a matter of Utnapishtim, the great father, ancestor of all, who stood before the gods in their Assembly, spoke to them of life eternal, and was given by them life eternal. I need to ask him about this life, and death.

Go, go then, Gilgamesh, through the Mashu and over the mountain, across the plain, down into the night Road of Shamash, may your feet go in safety, though you're blind as a mole. Go.

He followed the scorpion's heading. At one league there was no light...

...and at two leagues he still kept going...

...and at three, and four, pitch black, so he knew his going was right.

Five leagues and six, and he hurried, unable to see in front or in back.

TRIP!

THUD!

Seven, eight leagues in Shamash's tunnel, and still the darkness was whole.

He gave out a shriek.

Awful enough that Shamash heard, and bent down to him, a voice in the dark:

Gilgamesh, where are you going? This life you seek, that has no end, you won't find it here, you won't find it anywhere!!!

And Gilgamesh said to his valiant sun...

I've roamed the steppe, climbed the mountain, and now plow through a dark that's my own reward? Shall I sleep like this forever, my dank pillow the bowels of the earth?

I prefer thy light, warrior. Give me my fill of it, sate me with sun. The dead don't ask this of thee. I may be dead, but I'd have thy rays.

And he trudged on, and at nine leagues, nine double-hours of darkness, came a wind! The North Wind lapped at his face...

WWHOOOOSHH!!

...but dense was the darkness, light there was none.

Leaves of lapis lazuli, vines of something vermilion, briars of agate and horn. The jasper, jade and bright topaz, incarnadine banks of radiant rubies, spilling down to an emerald sea — his eye is fooled: he blinks, stares out on an emerald, yet tossing, a green and watery sea!

Down by this sea lives an ale-wife, the keeper of a tavern... for whom?

On the tables the jugs are of gold; out back, her beer ferments in huge golden vats... forged by whom?

She wears a veil; Gilgamesh in lion skins, plods wearily toward her—mayhap the flesh of the gods on his body, but woe still flush in his heart.

He looks like one who has traveled past nowhere, from beyond nowhere he comes.

From her distance she watches his plodding, his bent head a'nodding—

This is not good, she thinks. This one's a bandit or madman, or worse, some killer perhaps; I'm not safe.

She slides the bolt in her door. Gilgamesh hears it click home, painfully raises his chin, sees her lurking within.
Tavern maid!
KNOK! KNOK!
CLAK!

Ale-wife, one look at me and you bar your door? I heard the bolt! You want me to walk through it now? Open, or I'll smash my way in.

Then he begins to babble—the troubled ghosts on the plains, and some gates, a door, a man named Gilgamesh.

And she, the ale wife Siduri, lets him in...

...sits him down, lets him talk.

He would be Gilgamesh, destroyer of monstrous Humbaba, lumberjack of the Cedar Forest, killer of lions, fabulous bull fighter — a heavenly fire-breathing bull, if you will - they struck him down, too, he says.
GLUG GLUG

You hear such stories in taverns, down by your emerald sea, though not always from just one lone traveler, under one adventuresome name.
So you are Gilgamesh. Killer of the guardian of the Cedar Forest, slayer of lions, butcher of the Bull of Heaven — You look so bad I almost believe it.
GULP!

Gilgamesh felt at her hand on his beard.
You are quite battered. Your cheeks are caved in, your face is a battleground — this army certainly lost!

But lion skins in this weather? For the wild man of the steppe it will do, but this man before me's no animal — your eyes! This here poor man... is wretched!

How far have you come? If you really are he, father of all these marvelous triumphs, why so entirely battered, whence such monstrous grief?

My cheeks should be battered. How could they not, how could I not look like a carcass, drying stiff in the sun? A carcass, yet with a heart pumping woe.

I had a friend, loved him more than myself, we did all things, together—

In the grip of giant Humbaba once, in tears, saying our farewells—

Ha! We slew that ogre instead.
DONK
DOOK
THUMP

We did all things together until mortality struck.

He stopped and turned from the window to look at Siduri.
Enkidu he was. I mourned him for a week. I would not let them bury him...

...until a worm dropped from his nose.

And now that worm pursues me! Barmaid, I fear Death, so I roam.
THUD
CLANK

In the company of ghosts, stepping carefully between the words of my dying friend. I failed him once, it drags me down—could I have saved him, did it kill him, my cowardice?

How can I not roam, how can I now be silent?

Gilgamesh indeed.
SNIFF!

The one that I loved has turned to clay. Clay cannot chase the panther, the wild ass on the steppe.
Humbaba, the mountain, the goddess... can clay offend omnipotent gods?

Can clay be love? My young brother—shall he, shall I... be clay? Like him, curl up in a lump forever? I've come into this world for this?

And this lovely face, having seen it, let me not see it, the death that I dread.

Gilgamesh, trust me, you won't find what you seek. There is no point to your wandering, it cannot quench this thirst for life everlasting. The glorious gods, they created mankind, but with life they also gave death. Gave it away, keeping eternal life safe in their unearthly clutches.
BLUP
BLUP

Now there's an answer to this: it's your stomach. Your liver, your heart and your skin. Attend to these!
TEE-HEE
HEH!
POINK!

Here, drink, eat, fill up thy stomach. Tonight, take pleasure, tomorrow, take pleasure. Look about—all these happy inconsiderate things. Peel back their secret: today's a holiday!

It's all a holiday, when you live. Invite people to your party, dance with them, laugh, dance in your heart—put on some clothes! Fresh linen, imagine, caressing this skin.

As for that, and clean hair, take the wee child by the hand—can you see it? It's yours, it's you, it's eternal- -not this!

In god's name, let me give you a bath! A wife would delight in your embrace, take joy in your lap. This, Gilgamesh, is how man, and also woman, live life.

And think you he'll be glad to see you, Urshanabi, the boatman? Him and his magical stones—they must be perfect, picked from the woods—without their balance no one can pull across.

When Gilgamesh heard this, he grabbed up his axe, snatched his dagger from its sheath, and leaped, whirling and flailing. Like an arrow shot among lions he fared out on the road...
CHOP!
HACK!
...he attacked his long journey, kept lunging and hacking, how many days?
His racket was heard. Urshanabi came running, dodging the blows, striking his head with his fist.
NOOOOOO!!
Most distraught, out of breath—beating his chest and thighs, while Gilgamesh hacked...
BONK!
KRASH!
TWUD!
...Chopping through vines, shattering stones there at the shore, beside the Waters of Death!

Who are you?!
CRASH!
SNAP
KRK

I am Gilgamesh, from Uruk, of the House of Anu, and have wended my way through the mountains, from sunset to sunrise through Shamash's tunnel, to seek Utnapishtim, the Faraway.

Of what use is that to me? I am the Faraway's ferryman. You would cross to the Underworld? You cross it only with me, Urshanabi, the boatman.

Here on my side, the living; over there, the dead.

But you look half dead already, like you've journeyed more than is human. Your face, it looks frozen and burned. Why do you roam? Why is your body in ruins?

Man's fate has overtaken Enkidu among the dead. And now, now that I've seen your face, I will see that of Utnapishtim. Ferryman, take me.

You see those broken stones? There's your ride, you fool. Those creeper vines you hacked to pieces — shall I haul my boat now on braided water snakes? You've destroyed all crossings with your axe.
Then tell me the way! If I can I will cross that sea; if not, then I'll roam. My friend's made of clay.

Gilgamesh, take thy restless axe, go down to the forest and hew you twice sixty poles—

...no, make that two hundred—or maybe three. We'll need three.

And each should be thirty meters: You don't want your hand in that sea. Then trim these punting poles, and cap each with a knob of bitumen, and then bring the bundles to me.

Hearing this, Gilgamesh drew forth his hatchet, climbed down through the woods, cut and fashioned the poles;
CHOP!
WHUK!
HAK!

Soon, with the three hundred poles in his arms, he returned to the boat.

And they boarded, cast off, slid out over the water, Urshanabi at rudder, Gilgamesh planting each pole, heaving long, leaving it sticking up behind.
"Do not touch the water," Urshanabi kept saying.
The knob, push from the knob! The water is death!

The boat rowed low, but smooth and intent like a mythical creature, leaving a trail of zigzaggered poles behind.
I call her The Magillu. We glide like a marsh hen, but I fear we run low on the poles.
HiiSS!
FZZT!
PSHHT!
FSHIZZLLE!
BOORSHT
SiZZLE!
SKXZTZ!
GLUG! GLUG!

UMPH!
SPLUP!
FSSZT!

GRUNT

HUP!
SPLASH!

FZT!

Three days Gilgamesh punted, covering a month and a half, but the number of poles had dwindled, reaching all the way back in their path.
HISSS

Gilgamesh reached for the last one: it was already out there behind. Poling was done.
PZZZSCH!

He stripped off his skins, held them aloft like a sail, put himself in the bow like a mast.
FLUP!
FWAP!

On the shore they approached, Utnapishtim sat up and gazed out at the offing, and mused to himself:
What sort of sails are these — why sails at all? Where are the stones of the rope-ferry, where indeed is the rope!? In the bow, all billowy wings — this is not my boatman, this man is none of mine, and what is that...?
SPLUP!
LAP!

Before the boat even touched, Utnapishtim called questions:
You, haggard one, how far have you come?
SYZSLZK!
FWUSHHHH!!
Aieee!

I can guess, it's all on your face, every rut's in your cheeks: your heart's on your sleeve and your cloak's dragged through keen winter and drought!

And this, what's left of a lion skin? Looks more like the pelt of a shoat.

And Gilgamesh, somewhat distracted, but used to such questions, gave out his name, began his retort: And should he not look so wretched, seared by the bright stinging heat, bruised by the cold that burns?
♪
!
?
SKERTCH!
FWUUUUHH!

His friend the panther, the wild-ass hunter, the one with his foot on the throat of Humbaba, the one who dragged the Bull to the ground, slew lions with only his hands — the one who could not wake from his fate —
My friend! — now king to a city of worms!
!!!!
SPLOOSH!

I follow him, I fear in my bowels that I *will* follow him: so I roam the vast distances, bearing his blame, seeking to lighten my burden, seeking for quickness in clay.
PHEW!
WHUD!
TRIP!
GWUSH!

Thus I set forth to find Utnapishtim, this one they call Faraway. Indeed, he's well-named.

I've crossed all over this land — how many kingdoms, how many rivers and seas, the endless turbulent mountains, until one woe yoked my heart to my knees.

I've slept very little. This face you see of a carcass, unsweetened by sleep. These sinews that ache, that bite at each step... These cumbersome shoulders...

Imagine the ale-wife: my clothes all but gone. I've been living on bear meat, what game that I'd killed — a lion, hyena and deer, one wild boar. A goat from the rocks. The raw skins of these animals were all that I wore.

She bolted her door against me! But you can't bolt your door against grief, seal it up with pitch and bitumen, or find relief in games and gay capers — there are no more games, there is no more dancing...

Why do you feed on this grief?

To be made from the flesh of the gods is a wonderful thing — but the flesh of a man, quite another.

One of them — thy father, thy mother — left thee in part a mortal behest: Death for dear baby Gilgamesh, and death for his brother, and this village idiot I see here before me, he too will die...

... though he gird up his loins in uncured skins, though he feed on everyone's garbage, though he suffer and babble of sins.

You must think there's a spare chair in Assembly, for him wearing a tail for a sash. You dream of gods going sleepless because a man acts like a fool?

The gods are sleepless, Gilgamesh, or not, as they wish, and they're saving up crud, to serve you as butter. Chaff be your grain, they'll ordain, for your pains.

Tell me, where is thy gain? This unceasing toil, this cauldron of grief in your belly, this giving up sleep- what you're giving up is the life you have left!

Utnapishtim swept low with the edge of his hand. Then he pointed off into the air.
Like the reeds on the riverbank- cut at the root!
The fine youth, the beautiful maid- see them? And did they know, in their beauty, they would finally breed death?
WILT!
DROOP!
MEERP!

No... No one sees death.

No one looks for death's face, no one turns to death's voice, and yet-

His hand swept the ground once again.
...and yet it is savage!
SWUT
SLASH!

But I'm entertained, I've not talked in a while. Tell me, are you a builder of houses that last forever?

The meticulous contract, you sealed it with an eternal signet? The brothers, their families will live there forever, divvying shares for all time?

And the contenders, will enmity last so long? You see what I'm saying?
Uhh...

When the river rises, and the land is drowned, does the earth become sea everlasting?

The dragonfly flits on the river, darting off into the sun— it has always been so, am I not right?
FWAP!
FFFSHH!
VVVT!
SWIPE!

Will it flit before Shamash's face forever? Say yes? And what of the night?
BZZT!
SMEK!
VVVVWT!

But I prate, while your eyelids grow heavy as pitch.

My point is nothing's forever, certainly not staying awake—you need a bed!
YAWN!

But say I drew you a picture of such a one peacefully sleeping, and another utterly dead, do you think you could say which was which?

Servant or master, moron or monarch—when Aruru decrees with the Anunnaki what destiny's been allotted—that's when it ends, and therein lies your secret: the great gods grant both to us equally, death and life they decree...

...but the day of one's death is not given, it's decided later, right there in Assembly, but the end is the same, after me.
After thee?

I built the boat, cut the rope, rode the Flood—gad! the noise of a thousand bulls, like a wild ass screaming, aye!

The winds for a week—all was dark. The gods, at each other's throats. Enlil was furious, wanted no humans—too noisy, he said, while Enki defied him...

...and I, Utnapishtim, am not dead.

Ah! Since you ask, I will tell you, Gilgamesh, tell you of a hidden matter. This is a secret now, kept by the gods. I shall tell it to thee:

You know Shurrupak, on the banks further up the dark Euphrates from your kingdom of Uruk—as great a city as yours but far more ancient is my Shurrupak—the gods lived right there in our town! I was the priest, I was the king, they called me Ziusudra back then.

"Anu the father, and Enlil, valiant counselor, terrible warrior, and the herald Ninurta, and Ennugi, god of proper canals. All were there.
And also the wiley Enki, the one you call Ea, always our friend.
It came into their hearts to call forth a great flood. Anu pronounced it, but Enki demurred...
...he slyly divulged the terrible secret by whispering to the wall of a reed house:
Psst! Hey--
Reed house, reed house! Wall, wall! Better listen, wall. Understand me, house.

And this boat was to be built to specifications most odd, her length and her width were exact and the same, like a coffer, a towering box! And the roof, he said, make it like that of his own undersea temple. I took it all in but the obvious question:"

O, Far-sighted, O, great Trickster – consider it done. Indeed, it's an honor – but, lord, what of the people, what do I tell them? The elders aren't entirely stupid.

And, rid of me, you'll be showered aplenty, like a bounty of fowl—it'll darken the sky, like wheat pouring down from the heavens, or riches of fish spewing forth from your nets.

And what do you think saw the dawn, hey? Full teeming with people and tools—the carpenter's hatchet, the reed worker's stone, the children toting tar by the bucket; and the weak and the frail, stumbling along with whatever else they could bear!

On the fifth day I laid out her framework: the floor covered an acre! Six decks, the sides reaching up for dozens of cubits — ten dozen up, ten more across...

The thing was a cube, I tell you, more a bob than a boat, a square ziggurat he assured me would float!

Bulls I slaughtered daily, and sheep, and I ladled out wine as if it were river water.

It didn't seem like work, more like fun, the feasting at New Year's— the crowd and the beer and the mutton knee deep...

Not quite as easy to launch her— two thirds of her dry, we had to run rollers from aft to the bow, and she's loaded all wrong with everything possible.

Silver and gold—yes! I confess, all I could carry.
And the seed of the living—the animals, all of them, and the children and cousins, and dozens of craftsmen...
...the beasts of the field, the wild ones, too...
...and finally Shamash's careful instruction:
When he who brings the "grain" tonight sends rivers of it, crashing from the height, *then* board thy ship, and batten down tight!

Without a doubt, that hour'd arrived. It rained indeed like an abundance of "grain".
From morning to night came a sleet of "wheat". I peered smack into his face...

... the mad god in the storm; his monstrous billowy bounty was a terrible sight;
B-BAROOUMM!!
KKSSSHHHH!!
WWROOARRR!!
SPLIP!
PATTER!
SPLAT!
DRIP!
I scrambled aboard and sealed the hatch, tight.

I'd made my good-byes: to Puzur-Amurru who'd caulked the craft, for all his good work I gave him my palace!
The opulent palace and everything in it!

And just before dawn, out where the land meets the sky there grew such a menacing cloud, stupendous and black and towering, and Adad thundered within it, Shullat and Hanish preceding like heralds, flashing over the mountain, far out on the plain —
KKRAAKADOOOM!!
—the dome was cracking!

Erragal of the Underworld — went about yanking up pilings.
PWAUGHFFF!
CKAK!
GRNT!
WROOARRR!!
SPLASH!
BRRK!
KRUSHHH!!
CRASH!

Ninurta sprawled his warrior self out: the dikes overflowed like fountains!
BROOOSH!
SQUIRT!
PFWAAPHFF!
KRUK!
PFWAAPHFF!
CRUMBLE!
QKWUSH!

Astonished were the gods in heaven, at Adad's destruction, at his light-gobbling storm, at his raising the whole land up on high and smashing it down like a pot.

ZAP!

It blew for a day, it rushed over our heads with the force of a battle, unable to see the man right beside you. Even the gods looking down from heaven — they recognized no one.

BRKOW!

BOOOUUUUMM!

They fled! The glorious gods were appalled;
as frightened as we, they bolted for the skygod's top heaven —
Anu's outermost sphere, where they cowered like dogs at the base of a wall.

A shriek, like a woman in labor—Ishtar, whose voice is so usually sweet, was wailing: "O, Time, you've turned to drab clay! Because I spoke amiss? How could I say evil in Assembly, ordering ruin for my people—them I gave birth to, look, they float like white spawn, like a tide of dead fish."
KVTZK!
WHHWWUUUU¡¡¡¡UUU!!!!!
BKAW!

The Anunnaki wept, too, bowed their heads and sobbed, spittle caked on their lips. For a full week it blew, swept the land with shouldering flood, pounded with storm, these forces contending like huge struggling armies, like a woman writhing in labor...
VVFTZ!
BWUOARR!
CRASH!
ZZKAAK!
PKWFF!

...a seven-day labor, until...
...there was born a great calm: the sea became tranquil...
...the rain became quiet. The flood tides abated somewhat.

I pried open a crack...

...looked out at the weather: quiet and calm.
The sun poured over my face, gentle, serene, a beautiful day...
...except, my fellow man – turned completely to clay. All, everything, the land as the sea, as flat as a roof.

I pushed open the hatch: fresh air poured in with the warmth and the light.

I lowered my head, sunk to my knees and wept – such a sight! It still lingers.
SOB!

Tears streamed down my nose, soaked my cheeks, my own little flood – while here and there land was emerging, like a dawn but of mud, with gray slimy fingers.
I scanned the horizon for some solid shore, but saw only the points for surveying, the far mountains we use, all fourteen peaks – mere mounds in a desert of sea.
BRRUUTTCHH!
KRUNK!
But the ark was scraping: we were running aground. On Mount Nisir we stuck – it bumped and crunched, held fast, but I gave it more time.
A full week I waited...

...then, let go a dove...
FLAP FLAP!

...who returned the same day, nearly dead with exhaustion.
FLOP FLUP FWUP!

I tried a swallow...
FLUTTER FLUTTER!
Chirp!

...not strong enough, the land was too far.
FLIPPETY FLOP FWUF!
Gasp!

And finally a raven, who cawed and circled and soared, fed on the air...
BKGAW!
It did not return.

So I opened her up! Threw open the doors and let them all out: to the four winds, begone!
And then I made sacrifice, poured my libations on the top of the mountain, set tripods and kettles, fifty or more...
KLAK
DOINK!
BOING!
POK!
CHOMP!
HOP!
SPLASH!
GLUB!
...and I heaped up the cedar, myrtle and cane – the fragrance!

The gods smelled the sweet savor and gathered like flies, like a cloud of flies around a man making sacrifice, up to his elbows in blood.

Then, suddenly, the great goddess appeared, holding before her the necklace Anu had made when he'd courted her; draped through her fingers the columns of flies of lapis lazuli, as blue as her eyes, Belet-ili, Ishtar-as-Mother, came:

Ye gods, by this necklace of flies I shall remember. As surely as this lapis lazuli from my neck I always wear, so forever these days shall I bear. Let the gods approach this offering, but let not Enlil come near, he without a second thought, without a word to us—to bring on such destruction!

VWOOP!
FLASH!
BZZZZZ!
WHiiiiRRRR!
Vviiiiv!
BZWONT!

No sooner said than Enlil appeared, saw my ship, and was enraged. Through his teeth he railed against gods:

Ninurta piped up:

And then Ea made himself heard:
Warrior, wisest of all, how could you not consult us? How, alone, could you rouse up such waters? Lay the sin on the sinner, punish the wicked even with wickedness, but *this*... exceeds.

When the man wanders, pull him in; when that's too taut, give slack.

OOOWOOOO!
I would a great wolf had arisen, and culled the proud people down. A lion could come, and transgressors would wane. A famine! That would slaughter them nicely, instead of this flood.
ROARR!

A plague, imagine: Irra with his livid pustules could have lathed them all in blood.
Aw, shucks.

Anyway, it wasn't me, not I who divulged the gods' secrets. The wise one here merely saw a dream, the rest he did himself, having read our secrets well. So, decide now, what of Utnapishtim?

Then Enlil grabbed my hand and led me up onto the deck.
My wife, too, he brought on board, and made her kneel beside me.
There he stood between us, the Lord Wind, vexed, burning. He touched our foreheads, and through his teeth did bless us:
Utnapishtim, once human, now divine! Henceforth Utnapishtim, and his wife here, shall be like us, immortal. And he shall live in the faraway, where the heavenly rivers meet.
And they did take me far away indeed, to the source of the celestial rivers...

You there! Tell you what: for starters, let's see you go, what, a week? Let's see you go six days and seven nights without sleeping.

PONK!

ZIIP!

And so she did. And the loaves lined up, and the wall was marked, as Gilgamesh slept.
SNORK!
BZZXT!
DROOL!
SKRT!

And slept, and the loaf at the front of the line was dry as a cake.

The next one was crusty...

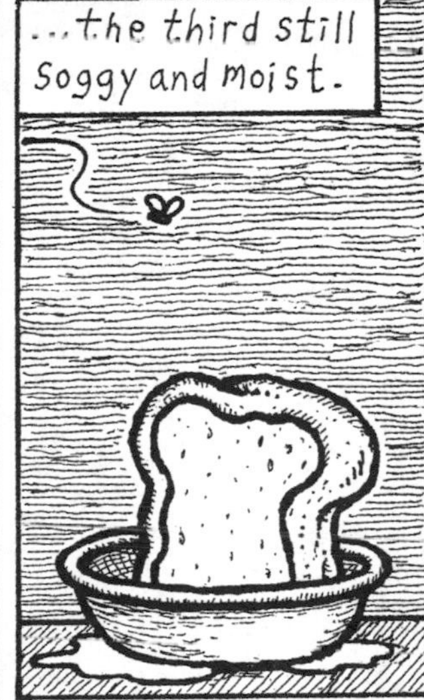
...the third still soggy and moist.

The fourth had grown a white beard...
BUZZZZ!

...while the fifth had turned lumpy and green.
VVVVM!
FLIT!

The sixth fairly stank...
BZZT
REEK!

...but the last, ah, still on the coals—Utnapishtim sniffed and said he was hungry...

MMM!

... and he shook Gilgamesh.
Ho... I'd just nodded off. Just dropped my head when you shook me.
Mm hm.

Look at your bread — a rainbow of bread going bad: this one is dry, this one leather, the third here is soggy. Count 'em!

Fresh bread sprouts not a beard...
Eew!

... neither white, nor... look at this one: a bubbly blue!
Yeeuck!
PLOP!

Count them, there lies the number of days you slept.

Utnapishtim, O, Faraway, what am I to do? Where can I go?

Before I can even turn, a thief has stolen my way. Death sits at the foot of my bed. Death stares back at me, leers at me from all things.

And this one you brought here—look at him, matted hair like a dead animal, and animal skins for raiment, marring his fine form—take him, take him to the washtub and cleanse that hair, make it shine. Throw those pelts into the sea.

B-bu-but!

... as the men made ready their boat, cast off, and pushed out to sea.
Good luck! Bon voyage!
FIZ

At the foot of the dock the Faraway's wife called out to her husband:
That man came a long way to see you and his journey was not easy— a gift was our custom once. What gift have you for his return?
Hush, woman.

Gilgamesh heard her and brought 'round the boat with his pole...
GRRRR!
...and with one heave, back to the dock they glided.

Your journey was work and great weariness, Gilgamesh. What gift should I make for your return?

I'll tell you a secret, a divine secret, familiar only to the gods.

He pointed:
Just there, out there on the bottom, grows a sweetwater plant, with thorns like a rose. It pricks! But if you can pluck it, and eat its flower, you will be young again, and lifelong.

Fast upon hearing that, Gilgamesh tied large stones to his feet...
...and pushed out over the current...
BRAK!

...to slide down under the sweetwater river—

...the stones dragged him down...
PLOOOSH!
SPLUB!
BLUB!
GLUG!

...down to the bottom...
BLUB!
BLOOP!
BLUP!

...where the plant held fast.
PLOIK!
FLIT!
GLOOT!
GLUB!

And though it pricked him deep,
he plucked it...

...then cut the stones from his feet...

... and the sea spit him out on the shore. And Gilgamesh said to the boatman:
Urshanabi, this is a plant like none other, the mother of breath, the killer of death, a plant that makes old into young! And I, I will take it to Uruk: that the elders partake of it, and so may I, in my time, become as I was in my youth!

And at ten double hours of poling, they ate from their store;
CRUNCH!
MUNCH MUNCH!

at twenty they put to shore...
#%@*!!
HUP!
SKRUUTCH!

... made camp for the night, inland, beside a deep pool...
... as cool, as quiet as it was dark.

And while Gilgamesh bathed in this pool, a snake moved, last light on its scales...

It seemed but one more root at the banks, yet flowing, slow, flicking its tongue, tasting the fragrant scent of the plant.

It slithered in silence to where the plant lay, and seized it, and carried it off...

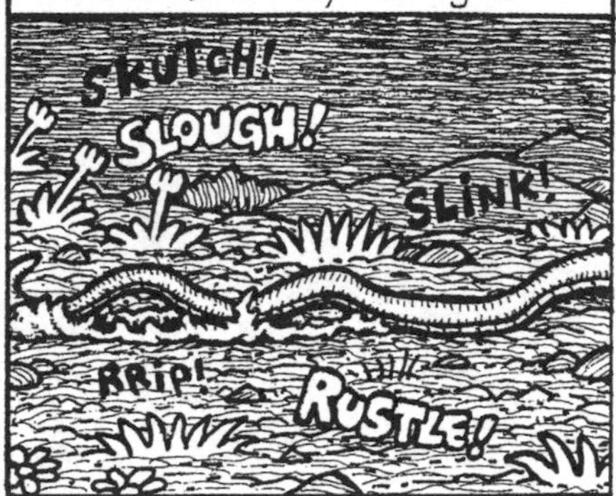
... Snaking away, leaving its skin behind: its very skin peeled off. It shed its scaly old age!
SKUTCH!
SLOUGH!
SLINK!
RRIP!
RUSTLE!

And Gilgamesh came and stared down at the skin, and sunk to his knees and wept, the tears flowing over his cheeks, like the spring caressing the rocks.

Why, Urshanabi?! Why have these arms worked themselves weary? Tell me, lest my heart break, for whom has my blood run its course? I have gained nothing! My boon for a slithering lizard, I've given all to a groveling snake.

I know a sign when I see one. My chance was out in the channel, and now we're twenty leagues off.

Let the boat sit, let us strike landward, and have done with the mystery of death.

I quit.

And at twenty leagues more they broke their fast...
MUNCH!
CRUNCH
SNARF!
CHEW!
SMAK!
GLOM!

...and at thirty stopped for the night.

Came then the light of day and not long...

...not long before great Uruk rose into sight. Uruk of the Sheepfold, and in the valley before it-
Gilgamesh the Shepherd.

See the walls, my friend? Do not its burnished bricks shine like copper?

Go on, approach, lay your hand against its mass, climb up upon it and inspect its ramparts. You'll say the Seven Sages were its masons.

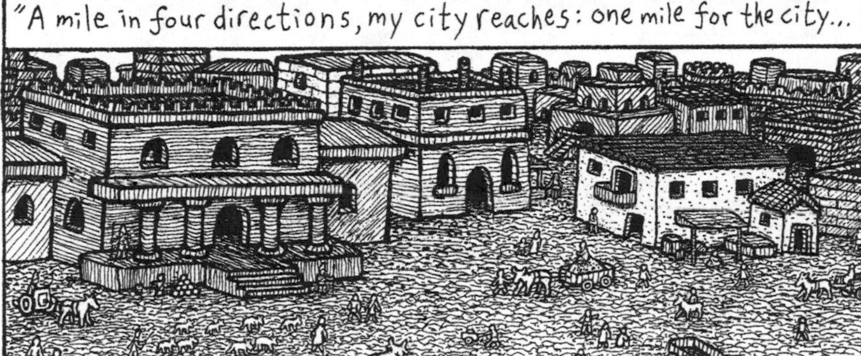
"A mile in four directions, my city reaches: one mile for the city...

...another all of orchards...

...a third square mile, the claypits...

...another half again for Ishtar's holy temple and her joys."

My kingdom covers, as a lover, three miles and a half of glory...

But then he bowed his head into his hands and said so none could hear:
I but dream, Enkidu. I dream of naught but toys.

Yet another night the old king tossed and dreamed away —

if only he'd left the pukku in the carpenter's house that day!

The pukku knot from the *huluppu* tree, and the striking stick...

ZZZZZ!

SNORK!

And the carpenter's wife, why comes she there in the thick of his dream?

My pukku's come to rest at the foot of Ganzir just there, at the eye of the netherworld, the first gate there.

PUK!

PUK!

PUK!

And my strong striking stick, my mekku, how came it to tumble after?

O, who will fetch my pukku, my mekku, up from the Underworld?

Came then Enkidu, somehow now his servant.
Master, your heart is sick? Why are you weeping?

I will fetch your pukku straightaway, your wood ball and stick...

...I'll bring them up from the Underworld this very day!

This day? Now, today? If you will go down today, down to the dim nether world, then you must heed what I say. I will instruct you in nays:

Have none of clean clothes, my friend—nay, wear nothing pressed nor clean! They will see right off you are a stranger there; they will mark your alien boast.

Nor anoint yourself—no scented oil from the jar: they will flock to its fragrance.

Brandish no weapon, shake no spear; anyone struck will crowd you and blow a storm in your ears.

Don't even carry a staff, or they will flutter about you: you'll spook a covey of ghosts.

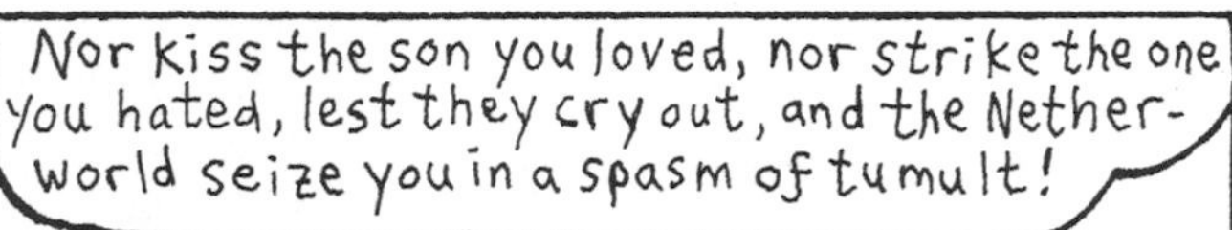

And she who sleeps and sleeps, Queen of the Netherworld, clattering her nails like a drum—At the end of the road of no return...

...where travelers dwell in darkness—dust their food, clay their bread, draped like birds in feathers. She yanks her hair like weeds.

But Enkidu heeded not his master.
He made the descent, in cleanest linen—
—and they knew.

He lathered himself in ointment, and they gathered to its scent.

He shook a javelin and the shades did quake;
He raised his club, they flocked and fluttered...
...waxed wroth at his sandals, the slap and scrape.

The wife once loved, he kissed...

...and smacked the one he'd hated.

The son he loved, he kissed...

...and struck the one he'd never loved—

—and the Netherworld cried out, and seized him...
...and behold—

And she who sleeps the sleep of dreams, Ereshkigal, sister of Ishtar fair, mother of Ninanzu, sleeping there, her shoulders bare and pale as ivory;

her breasts — unclothed, exposed, inviting as a jar of unguent —

Uneasy sleeps, moans, and, like as to the greeny leaves of leeks,

she tears away her hair.

it was the Netherworld welled up and seized him, the earth in loud upheaval.

RRUMBLE!

POK!

QUAKE!!

KRAK!

BKOW!

CRASH!

BAP!

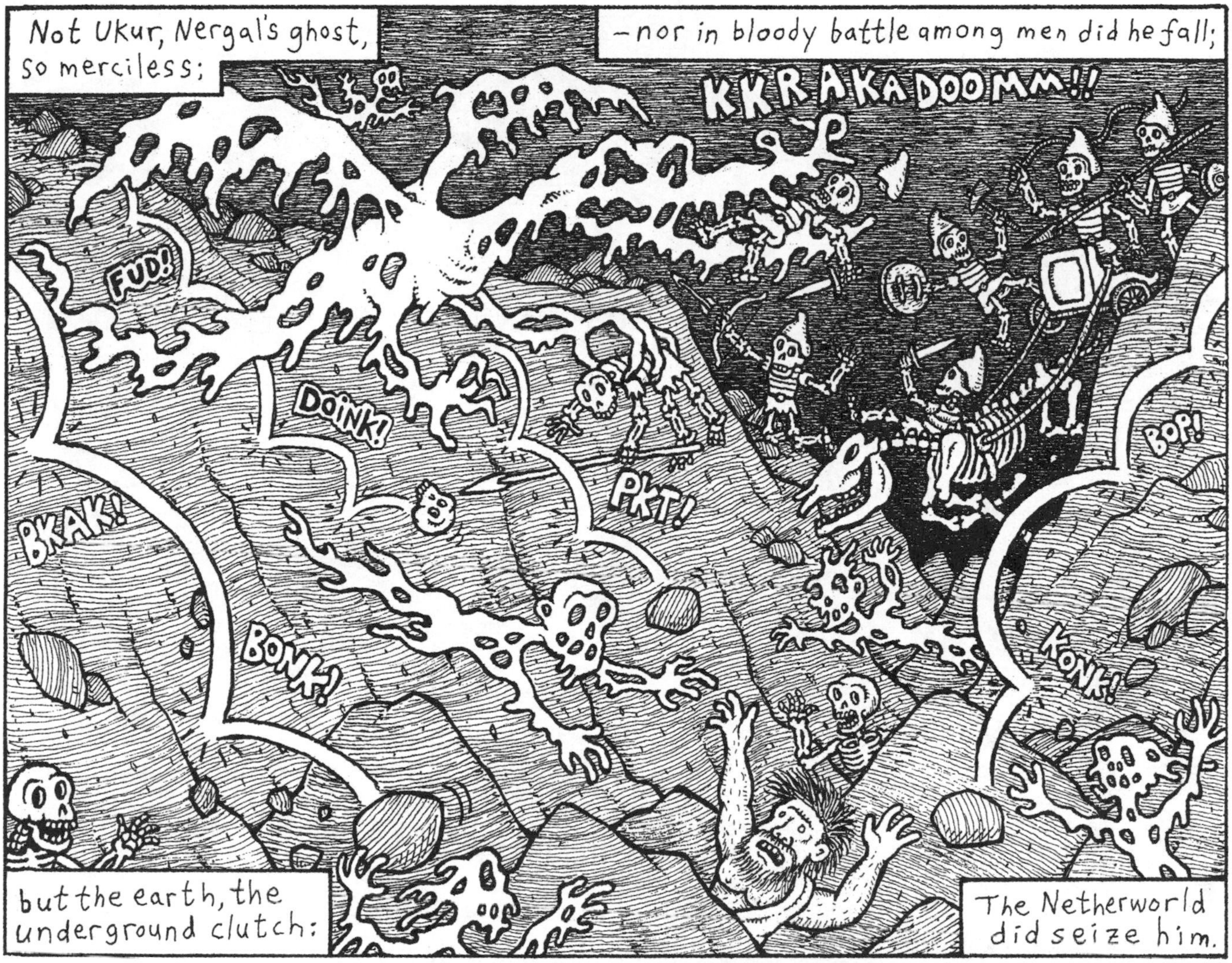

Not Ukur, Nergal's ghost, so merciless:

–nor in bloody battle among men did he fall;

KKRAKADOOMM!!

FUD!

DOINK!

PKT!

BOP!

BKAK!

BONK!

KONK!

but the earth, the underground clutch:

The Netherworld did seize him.

...Lord Gilgamesh tossed and wept for his old companion Enkidu...
...his friend that slept with no waking. He wept and cried to the moon:
O, Sin! My pukku, my mekku, they fell into the earth, and Enkidu went down after, and the Underworld has seized him.
And Sin answered not, not a word, and made his face a stone.

So to Ekur...
...the house of Enlil, Gilgamesh went alone.
My friend died not in battle, nor of disease. No plague swept him away; I sent him, he went, they seized him... he should walk with me today!

But Enlil answered not a word.

And so to Ea's temple...

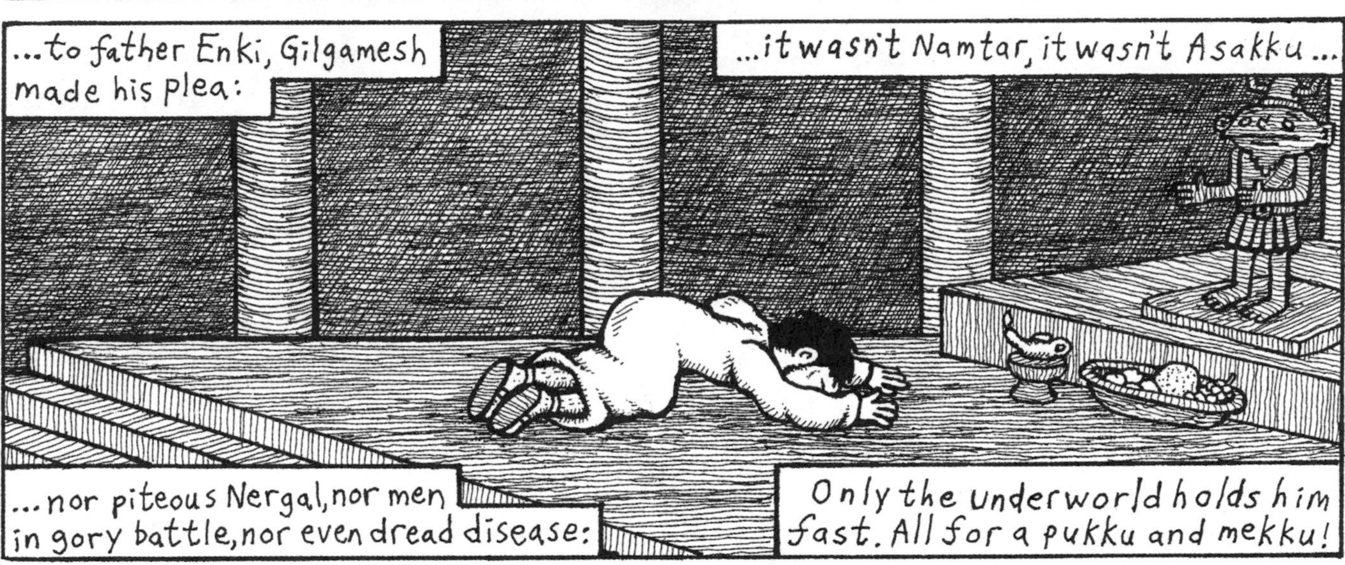
...to father Enki, Gilgamesh made his plea:
...it wasn't Namtar, it wasn't Asakku...
...nor piteous Nergal, nor men in gory battle, nor even dread disease:
Only the underworld holds him fast. All for a pukku and mekku!

And hearing this, lord Enki took his side and addressed the warlike Shamash.

Valiant Shamash, in your nightly journey under could you not poke a small hole in your tunnel, punch a wee rift in the earth for the shade of Enkidu, that his spirit may return from that darkness, to enlighten his brother Gilgamesh, on such as it is in the Underworld?

And Shamash harkened and straight away the earth did rend, whereupon the ghost of Enkidu flew forth like a whispering wind.
RUMBLE!
BRRUK!
CRAK!

They reached to embrace, they tried to kiss- they sighed, they blathered:
–O my friend, my friend, tell me, beloved friend, what of the ways of the Underworld? O, tell me what you have seen!

My friend, I will not tell you. If I told you, you would sink down and weep.

Then will I weep now. I will sit here and weep.
Sit then, for I will tell you, and you shall weep. Weep for this:

This form that you see, a body that once touched yours, knew the gladness of flesh like yours.

Worms consume it, shred and devour it, like a garment infested.

This body, my friend, whose bliss was your joy, whose pain was your hurt, lies moldering low, rife with vermin, and filled with dirt.

Gilgamesh cried woe, and threw himself down on the ground.
Whom have you seen? Did you see the man with one son?
I did.

And how does he fare?
Like a dog at the base of the city wall, a wimpering dog.

And the man with two sons, you have seen him?
I have. He sits on some bricks and sorts crusts with a stick.

And three, him with three?
Yes, I have. He drinks cool water from a skin.
SQUIRT!

And four?
He with four sons yokes four asses to his cart, and is glad.

And five sons, have you seen him with five?
I have. Like a fine scribe he is open-handed, trustworthy, he enters the palace most easily.

And the man with six sons, him you have seen?
Him I have seen, gliding his plow as through a field of loam.

And you saw him who had seven sons?
I saw.

And he fares...?

He fares as a man in a chair, placed among gods, with music for air.
And him with no sons, no heir at all, you saw him with the dead?
I saw.
And how does he fare?
He gnaws on a brick, calling it bread.
CRUNCH!
KRK!

And King Gilgamesh tossed in his bed.

The eunuch, the leper, the child still-born...

... the barren, the frigid, the wife bearing falsehood...

... or the man marked as a liar, or the one lost in battle, slain on the field...

...or him tossed aside, with no one to bury him—

And your leper has food and also slurps water, and lives off by himself...

...and the eunuch leans in a corner, like a brave ceremonial standard...

...and the liar—his lies make his skin shake like an ox's, Gilgamesh—not shivering at flies, but from worms that gnaw at his flesh.

And him cursed by mother and father, what of him, how does he fare?

He lacks an heir, and with no one to care, he wanders... elsewhere.

And the brave warrior, brought down in combat, what then of him?
His mother and father hold his head gently, while the tears of his wife pour off her chin.

And him who is homeless, has no one to mourn, no one to care?
Ill does he fare: his meat is scraps from the pot slung out in the street.

And the one never found, left dead on the steppe?
I saw him not. His spirit is restless, a mean ghost on the steppe.

The one set on fire, then, consumed in sharp flames?
He's not to be seen: his spirit shrouded in smoke, is lost in the sky. He's not to be seen in the world down below, not ever.

O, Enkidu, old friend, faint ghost: what of my children, the ones born dead, who never knew life, or muscle, or sweet water, or warm bread?
They play, Gilgamesh. They play at a table of silver and gold, laden with honey and butter twice-mulled.

!?!!

Whereupon he sat up: the dream had receded.
He who saw everything, saw his tablet completed.

BIOS

KENT H. DIXON is primarily a prose writer, but has published in all genres, including poetry and screenwriting. His fiction and nonfiction have been published in *Iowa Review*, *TriQuarterly*, *Shenandoah*, *The American Prospect*, *Georgia Review*, and *Antioch Review* among others. Recent translations include Mallarmé's *L'Après-midi d'un faune* and Rilke's "Leichen-Wäsche." In collaboration with Japanese students, he has translated previously unpublished *hibakusha* (A-bomb survivor poetry) in *Luna: Journal of Poetry and Translation*, *Wittenberg Review*, and elsewhere. With his artist son Kevin, he created the opening graphic novel excerpt of *The Epic of Gilgamesh* in editor Russ Kick's 2012 three-volume anthology *The Graphic Canon*. Kent was educated at University of North Carolina, Chapel Hill, with graduate degrees from Johns Hopkins University and a Ph.D. from University of Iowa—the Writers' Workshop. He teaches Creative Writing at Wittenberg University in Springfield, Ohio, where he lives with his writer wife. To read more of Kent's work, visit www.kenthdixon.com.

KEVIN H. DIXON is known for the autobiographical series . . . *And Then There Was Rock*, " . . . true stories about playing in a crappy loser band." With collaborator Eric Knisley, he produced *Mickey Death in the Winds of Impotence*, for which they won a Xeric Award. Kevin has done cover art for small presses in Chapel Hill, NC; run comic series in local newspapers; hosted "underground" talk radio shows; and contributed the cover to the first volume of *The Graphic Canon*, an *Oliver Twist* for the second volume, and a Brothers Grimm tale for *The Graphic Canon of Children's Literature*. Kevin lives in Chapel Hill with his wife and their three cats. To see more of Kevin's work, visit www.kevinhdixon.com.

RUSS KICK is the originator of the *Graphic Canon* series, for which he has commissioned new work from over 350 artists and illustrators, now going into its sixth volume. NPR described it as "easily the most ambitious and successfully realized literary project in recent memory." Kick's previous anthologies, *You Are Being Lied To and Everything You Know Is Wrong*, informed a whole generation of Americans with the hard truths of American politics and created a media frenzy for being the first to publish suppressed photographs of American flag-draped coffins returning from Iraq. The *New York Times* dubbed Kick "an information archaeologist," *Details* magazine described him as "a Renaissance man," and *Utne Reader* named him one of its "50 Visionaries Who Are Changing Your World." His popular website, thememoryhole2.org, is active again and getting national media coverage for archiving documents that the Trump administration has been deleting.